HANN
CREW

E.J.
Johnson

TURNER PUBLISHING COMPANY
Paducah, Kentucky

Turner Publishing Company

Copyrigt ©2000 E.J. Johnson
Publishing Rights: Turner Publishing Company
All Rights Reserved.

Library of Congress Number: Reserved

ISBN: 978-1-68162-405-1

Editor: Bill Schiller
Designer: Herb Banks
Cover Design: Shelley Davidson

Additional copies may be purchased directly from Turner Publishing Company.

TABLE OF CONTENTS

DEDICATION

"HANN'S CREW"

This book is dedicated to Ray E. Hann, our pilot, shown above in a P51 fighter plane. He was a fine pilot who got us all through World War II over Germany. His diary of our missions was duplicated and sent to each of the living crewmembers after the war. He graciously authorized the use of that data for this book, which is authentic. Thanks, Ray!

E.J. Johnson, Jr.

AUTHOR'S COMMENTS

My book is based on actual happenings leading up to, and during, World War II. I was drafted into military service and was qualified for acceptance in the Army Air Corps. After my graduation from Navigation School as an officer, I was assigned to the 8th Air Force along with the other people who came to be known as "Hann's Crew."

The period was 1944 and 1945, the time when our military efforts to defeat Germany were at their highest level. This began with the Allies invading the beaches at Normandy on June 6, 1944, known as "D-Day." The war ended on May 8, 1945 – "V.E. Day", which stood for Victory in Europe.

By April and May 1944, the 8th Air Force had built up to a level of approximately 200,000 personnel. Along with that, a tremendous increase in bombers and fighter planes had occurred, leading to 1,000 plane raids on most targets. Published reports stated that as many as 2,000 bombers and 1,000 fighters were assembled for these "Maximum Effort" raids in some instances. This hastened the collapse of Germany and war's end.

These developments represented the major efforts exerted by the people of the United States to overcome the disaster of Pearl Harbor on December 7, 1941. What an accomplishment in the 30 months between, and our capabilities by mid 1944!

CHAPTER 1
PRELUDE TO MILITARY ACTIVITIES

On November 28, 1923, there was apparently some discussion as to what I would be called... the night of my birth. My father suggested that "Joe" might be appropriate, but my mother had different ideas. She was emphatic that no son of hers would be known as "Joe Johnson" since there was a bootlegger of that name in the area of Pensacola, Florida, where we lived at that time. In retrospect, I thank you, Mom, for your wisdom. I was christened as Emanuel Joseph Johnson, Jr., but my family called me "Jimmy", a nickname given to my father when he was a youngster. I have been called *Jim* or *Jimmy* ever since.

We lived in Pensacola until 1935, the period of worldwide destitution. In the United States, banks were closed for some time as business activities had collapsed. No one had any money, unless he were wealthy and had funds stashed away *somewhere*. Most people were out of work, and those who had a job were very lucky indeed. My father was employed by the County, so he had a job. However, their payrolls were based on available funds being paid for taxes and other municipal type activities. The cash flow came in dribbles, so the employees had no regular payment schedule. I remember Dad coming home sometimes with five or ten dollars, which was a lot of money in those difficult days. However, I can also recall that when we moved to Charleston that year, his back payments due for the time he worked there came in to him for almost a year to complete paying him. That seemed to say that times were still hard everywhere.

Throughout the country, people were searching for any chance to make some money. Men "rode the rails" from east to west, north to south looking for employment. These people were known as "hobos", but they were really folks just down on their luck. When the trains came through Pensacola, these transients wandered the streets, looking for something to eat. They always went around to the back door, knocked, and asked if they might have some food. They were always polite, and were helped wherever the property owner could do so. In those days, no one ever thought to lock their doors, and thefts were rarely heard of. (In the 1990's era, one wouldn't dare open the door to strangers because you could be robbed or killed. What a tragic change in the way we now have to live!) The interesting thing about the transients was that they had some code, or sign, used to distinguish houses where food was likely to be available. I never found the answer, but few of them bothered to go to many houses, so it was evident they knew the best areas.

In 1935, my father had the opportunity to move to Charleston, South Carolina, where a paper mill was under construction, and the contractor needed someone to handle purchasing of materials for the project – and they paid weekly – in cash! Charleston was a very interesting place to live. At that time, I was just entering high school and went to Charleston High. It was quite different from Pensacola, and I was delighted to walk about a mile each way to and from school. We remained there until the fall of 1936, when Dad was offered a better job at a place named Fernandina, Florida, where two paper mills were under construction at the same time.

This flurry of construction of paper mills resulted from a study done by a concern in Savannah, Georgia, to determine if the southern pine trees could be used in the production of paper products. If my memory is correct, a process was developed by the Herty Foundation, and this opened the way for operating paper mills throughout the southern part of the United States.

The first paper mill under construction was then known as Kraft Corporation, I believe. Their product was brown Kraft paper, used for the production of corrugated boxes and other similar materials. The other mill was called Rayonier, and their production was dissolving cellulose, which was used by many plants for tire cord to manufacture automobile tires, films for cameras, as an ingredient in the manufacture of gun shells, and many other applications.

When we moved to Fernandina, it was a frontier town. The normal population was about 2,500 people, no houses were available for rent, unless some cottage at the beach, owned by out of state folks who used it for summer vacations, could be rented. The influx of personnel required for construction of the two mills was more than the regular inhabitants. As a result, tent cities sprung up among the sand dunes overlooking the Atlantic Ocean, tree houses sprouted up in several locations where beautiful old oak trees along a creek through the island were strong enough to support the structure, and one guy who owned a small chicken farm on the outskirts of town decided he could make more money by partitioning the hen houses and renting the space to the new immigrants. He stayed full during the entire construction period.

Fernandina is on Amelia Island, which is on the East Coast of Florida, the northern most barrier island before crossing the boundary line into Georgia. This line of demarcation is at the center of the St. Mary's River, which feeds from Georgia into the Atlantic Ocean. At the south end of the island, there is a large expanse of water separating Amelia from the islands south of here, so in those days you really had to make an effort to get here! There was only one road leading from the island over to the mainland, with a draw bridge spanning the Amelia River. A railroad line paralleled the highway, with a railroad trestle to permit boats to ply the river north and south – that was it!

For those having a car, there was no problem. The streets were in place to move around, some of which were paved, and others covered over with oyster shells or, in a lot of cases, just packed down dirt. Anyone else either had to hitch hike, walk, ride a bicycle, or ride McJunkin's bus to reach Jacksonville, the closest nearby city, about 35 miles away to the south. The bus was actually a four-door sedan, sawn in half and elongated for additional seating capacity, which made round trips about four or five times a day. It served the purpose for transportation and stayed full most of the time.

My parents arrived in Fernandina to check out the situation and explore locating a place to stay, prior to my arrival later. They found a cottage at the beach and were happy to have it, even though there was no hot water, no heating, and the wind whipped through the clapboard exterior siding where gaps had developed over a period of time. This may have been a nice summer camping spot, but the winter that year happened to be very cold, and we nearly froze to death. I came into town late one afternoon on McJunkin's transportation system. What a shock!! All through the depression, no one here had any money, with bartering between merchants, doctors, auto repair and service stations, among others, as the medium for commercial functions. The only real source of income was the shrimping industry, which was started here. Their biggest problem was distribution to nearby markets, since shrimp spoil rapidly unless iced down, and in that era, the only solution was to pack the back of a closed truck with ice and hope it didn't melt until destinations were reached. But, at least those involved did produce some revenue.

Obviously, the city had no money either, so the block wherein McJunkin's "Bus Station" was located, just adjacent to the Amelia River, had been pretty neglected and grass had grown up between the bricks in the street to a height of 3 or 4 feet. The only clear area was where McJunkin came in on one side, made a U-turn, and stopped on the opposite side. This large U was very prominent. One of the primary problems at Fernandina in those times was food, and where to eat. There were a few very small grocery stores, but their inventories couldn't meet the demands. Many people moving in to existing cottages didn't have facilities for cooking, refrigeration, etc., and this also applied to the tent city groups. There were several small restaurants, but nothing really suitable for mass production to serve the demands. One place was Nell's Kitchen, on the outskirts of town, where everything was good – hamburgers, sandwiches, fried shrimp, deviled crab, French fries, and salads, all of which were in great demand – but this was only one place for dining.

Several women got together and started a boarding house type operation, which was swamped every day. They had a good location in the downtown area, but one block off of the main street. The building they operated from was very small and may have had as much as 1,000 square feet, but it stayed busy.

Every room except the kitchen was equipped with some home made tables and benches on each side for seating. About twelve people could be seated at each table. Good old fashioned southern cooking was the order of the day – fried chicken, baked ham, collard greens, green beans, spinach, creamed potatoes, iced tea, coffee, etc. Every table had platters which were kept full as patrons came in and went out so someone else could sit down. Meals started about 4:30 p.m. when workers at the mills began to get off, and from that time until about 9:30 p.m., there were two lines of people waiting to get in. One line covered a city block in one direction, and the other stretched around the corner. These women worked very hard, to be sure, but they were a Godsend to hundreds of people, and I suspect they hit the jackpot with the right business in such trying times.

Through the next three years, things were up and down. Lingering signs of the depression forced delaying of construction for the two mills, forcing many people to leave in search of other job opportunities. Some semblance of business activity had been achieved with the circulation of money, in lieu of the earlier bartering program, and the city was able to establish a budget of $25,000 for the annual cost of operating during the fiscal year.

While all this was going on, I was going to high school. In June 1940, I was in the graduating class at Fernandina High school – we had about 14 in that group! I was sent to Georgia Military College, more commonly known as GMC, which was located in Milledgeville, Georgia, the original capitol of Georgia before it was relocated to Atlanta. This first year of college was not something I liked – the cadet routine with stiff rules for barracks study periods, time for lights out, military drills, and regimentation were not my cup of tea, but it turned out some good lessons for me later in life.

One night the building, formerly the Georgia State Capitol, caught fire. All the cadets were pressed into action for removing all of the rifles stored in the basement. Fire trucks and residents of town all turned out to help. A group I had been assigned to work with was instructed to help a local gentleman piling rifles into the trunk and back seat of his car for transportation to a safe place. Several of us piled into the car, and away we went, but at the end of the first block, we knew something was wrong! It developed that our friend couldn't see well at night, so we hung our heads out the windows to read signs, look out for oncoming cars, etc. When we finally arrived at the destination, we were in the Geor-

Taken just moments into the attack, this Japanese photo shows ship locations and Japanese planes in the middle and upper right-hand corner of the photo. Hickam field is burning in the background. (Japanese photo, courtesy of National Archives.

Smoke from the USS Arizona billows over the airfield at Hickam

gia State Insane Asylum! In view of all else, it seemed a fitting place to wind up, but how were we to know that a real human drama was taking stage across the world at the same time.

On December 7, 1941, Japan launched the most dastardly of sneak attacks against our forces stationed at Pearl Harbor. Franklin D. Roosevelt rightfully declared this as a "Day of Infamy," and our lives changed drastically. We were at war, caught flat footed, with our entire Naval fleet in the Pacific region practically destroyed. There was a tremendous loss of lives, and a desperate need to rebuild our resources of ships, planes, military facilities, and the complete litany of everything required for war, just to survive.

Pearl Harbor spawned scores of stories... some tragic, some inspiring, but all were accounts of genuine human sacrifice and service. One of the more notable stories involved the actions of Colonel Frank P. Bostrom of the 7th Bomb Group. Bostrom and five other B-17 pilots had been ordered to Hickam Field and arrived just in time to witness the attack at the height of its severity. Japanese fighters targeted Bostrom's aircraft, and despite receiving significant damage, Bostrom saved the lives of the crew by landing the B-17 on the 9th fairway of a nearby golf course. When the Air Corps Unit was notified, they made plans to dismantle the aircraft to better prepare it for transferring off the course. Bostrom, however, insisted that he could not only land, but that he could take off from that position by using the fairway as a runway. True to his word, he later touched down at the base in Hickam Field.

In a few short months, Bostrom's piloting skills were further distinguished when (as a member of the 19th Bomb Group) he was ordered to Mindanao and charged with the duty of safely evacuating General Douglas MacArthur and staff out of the country. A month later, Bostrom was the lead pilot on the General Ralph Royce Mission, considered the last bombing campaign of the Philippines before American forces, out numbered and under-supplied, were forced to surrender. Bostrom had flown dozens of missions by November, 1942, when he returned to the United States. He went on to serve as Commanding Officer at Bomb Group Training Command at Alamorgordo, New Mexico. I never could have guessed that my path would cross that of this extraordinary man.

As it was, the draft for military personnel

1st Lt. Frank Bostrom.
(Army Air Corps, 1940)

had been 21 years of age, but sometime in 1942, the age limit dropped to 18 years. Having just reached 19 years the prior November, I received notice to report to the Draft Board office along with all the others *called to duty.* There were 12 or 14 of us sworn in, with instructions to return shortly thereafter for transportation to Camp Blanding, Florida. Upon arrival there, we were processed as new draftees, given our physicals to determine who was in good enough shape to be in the Army. We got enough shots to protect us from any sickness likely to be encountered, each received an issue of GI clothes followed by our particular duty assignments. We were in the Army!

My first job was to wash down and clean out 30 gallon garbage cans. This meant that to be acceptable for Army use, the inside and outside had to be sparkling clean. Anything else was a "no-no" and could bring on very expletive comments from some character who had probably arrived a week before, and now thought he was a Master Sergeant! After a stint at this, I was promoted to "K.P. Duty." This entailed washing and drying large vats used for cooking, and stainless steel platters used to serve food and feed hundreds of GI's daily. The hours started about 6:00 a.m. and ended probably about 8:30 p.m. before all the kitchen and mess hall had been properly cleaned. The abrupt introduction to these job functions convinced me that I wanted to do something more interesting – and that did *NOT* include infantry warfare!

My initial step toward getting assigned to the Air Force was to request such a transfer. This was done at the Camp Blanding Headquarters, from which all troops were sent to various elements of the Army. Not knowing how this might work out, I fell back on an old adage when help is solicited- "It's now what you know, but who you know.". Fortunately, my Dad had been active in political circles in Northeast Florida, and his brother in Pensacola was involved State wide in assisting candidates running for the Florida governor's office. Three of these candidates were elected for four-year terms, and one of these Governors was later the senior Florida representative in the U.S. Senate, Washington, D.C., where he remained for many years. What, if anything, occcurred as a result of these contacts is unknown, but my objective for assignment to the "Air Force" came to pass when I shipped out to Miami Beach, for basic training in the Air Force. At that time in my life, this was the coldest place I had ever seen!

Because we had been sent to the mecca of Southern Florida, all of the uniforms issued to us were for summer wear. However, for drill practice, we had to march from our hotel overlooking the beach (and the hotel had no heat) to a park bordering Biscayne Bay. During the month of March, winds whipping across the bay were freezing cold, and our summer outfits did nothing to help keep us warm!

After about four weeks there, I boarded a troop train heading for Biloxi, Mississippi, to continue learning about Army life. Keesler Air Base was our new home for a while, and to accommodate the new troops pouring in, a number of the barracks had been built in a pine forest which was part of the base. These buildings were wooden construction, very low to the ground, and had plywood exterior covering. Each building probably had about 30 bunks. There were no windows as such, but screened openings were covered with hinged solid blinds which could be let down if the weather was cold. There were no other facilities, but we did have a latrine and shower building close by. It was here that I learned it was more important for me to have sleep in the morning, rather than some unappealing breakfast! Reveille was about 6:30 a.m., at which time it was still pitch black darkness on the outside. We were gathered in front of the barracks to "fall-in" for a review, which consisted of saying "present" when your name was called out, then heading for the mess hall. I soon decided to stay in bed. When my name was called, I'd look out through the screen and say "present" before rolling over and going back to sleep. The rest of the day was pretty rough with calisthenics, drills, etc.

Upon completion of our courses at Keesler, I boarded a troop train heading north, dropping off GI's at destinations along the way. Hundreds of troops were packed on board. Each carried his duffel bags full of clothes, personal items, and who knows what else. The railroad cars were usually equipped only with upright passenger seats, and very little space for storing the duffel bags. After stuffing as much as possible under the seats, the overflow was put in the aisle. Sleeping was something else again. In those days, there was no air conditioning on these cars, so the windows were open a lot of the time, permitting soot and cinders to infiltrate the interior, along with the passenger. As hot as it usually was, trying to sleep sitting upright, or lying on duffel bags in the aisle with people trying to step over you, was an interesting challenge. Meals generally were delivered to the train at stops along the way, and were comprised usually of sandwiches, cold drinks, etc. To say the least, these transitions were not like pleasure trips!

As the train made its way, I ended up in Omaha, Nebraska, for schooling at Creighton University, as part of our cadet training program. Since my records covered a year spent at Georgia Military College, Milledgeville, Georgia, training in military drills, etc., I was appointed as Cadet Commander! Quite a step upward, and it looked good on my personnel file. Creighton was a great place, with nice living accommodations in the dormitories, interesting and worth-while college courses which prepared us for later phases in our quest for graduation and wings, a wonderful football field for drilling practices, friendly townspeople, and great weather at that time of the year. The only small problem was that our cafeteria was quite a ways from the school,

CREIGHTON UNIVERSITY DAYS

Leading squadron for "on line" review by Senior Officers in charge.

Standing at attention before the squadron for Saturday afternoon Air Force officers review.

so three times a day all the cadets were assembled to fall in for the march to breakfast, dinner, and supper. To maintain the proper cadence for marching, we had many songs to sing, which everyone seemed to enjoy, including the homeowners along the way.

After several months, and completion of this training period, orders were issued which transferred the entire group at Creighton to Santa Ana, California. Having been the Cadet Commander previously, I ended up on this transfer as the Officer in Charge of the troop train. I had specific instructions not to lose any of the Cadets along the way! Now *that* was quite an order. Everyone had picnic packages to sustain them until our first stop. Troops debarked to run and find some fast food place for a hamburger or hot dog. For some cadets, this provided a perfect excuse to miss the train's departure and get lost... not my intention at all. Arriving at Santa Ana, we appeared to have lost three or four stragglers somewhere, but this was not a bad report considering the circumstances.

Our sojourn at Santa Ana lasted about three months, during which time we concentrated on more aspects of flying which, in turn, lead to preparations for Navigation school... all while continuing our body building routines, etc. It was somewhat different there, in that we seemed to have more liberty time to go into town, or to visit Hollywood. These experiences were interesting, but our Cadet pay of twenty-one dollars a month didn't go very far in that arena where dollars flowed like water! One of the less expensive

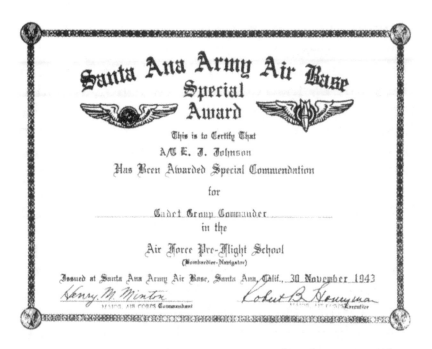

pastimes was to hang out at the intersection of Hollywood and Vine Streets, where a number of the movie stars passed.

Around the first of December, we were transferred to Hondo, Texas. It was there that I first saw snow, blowing down from the plains. This was the make or break part of our training. Here we studied every aspect of Navigation, and had tests so often no one ever knew if they were in or out of the program. Many of the Cadets couldn't keep up with the pace and were dropped. Those remaining were taken on test flights very frequently to check out whether they had learned what they were supposed to absorb in the classroom. There were about 6 students on these flights which would depart from Hondo and fly to Des Moines, Iowa, for instance, then back to Love Field at San Antonio, to complete the trip, and check the results of how the Cadets performed. The procedure was that one Cadet would be designated as the lead navigator for the trip north. He controlled the heading for the plane by instructions to the pilot, and also the "ETA" (Estimated Time of Arrival) at the destination. The other cadets did their own navigation, with their individual results compared to the lead navigator. The object was to get to the Des Moines airport, on time. Missing the target by 15 miles and 10 minutes was not acceptable.

On the return trip, another cadet took the leadership position, and the others followed the procedure outlined. Arriving at Love Field in San Antonio, comparisons for the first leg of the flight were compared to establish grade ratings for each cadet. Frequent test flights continued to weed out cadets and heightened the concern of those trying to graduate. There are a lot of different types of navigation. Each student had a map covering the area of flight from take off to arrival – these showed lakes, railroads, towns, etc. If you looked out the window and saw a railroad line heading toward the target and it was identified on the map, follow it as far as it might be helpful. Other landmarks, such as lakes, were excellent pinpoints to compare with your actual location. Radio signals from a specific location were sometimes very helpful – celestial equipment for a "shot" at the moon, or specific constellations of stars could be plotted on your chart to establish your location – anything which could be used was acceptable to get a passing grade – and that was the total objective! Those of us who passed the tests received our wings and commission as a Second Lieutenant in the Air Force. My group was known as the graduating Class of April, 1944, from the Hondo, Texas, School of Navigation. At that time, I had reached the ripe old age of 20.

Our first order of business after getting our gold bars as Second Lieutenants was to find officers' clothing. The Air Force furnished clothes only to enlisted personnel. Officers therefore, were responsible for meeting their own requirements. Fortunately, there was a bank in Hondo where graduates could get a loan. I borrowed $150.00, which was enough to buy basic uniforms to clothe me for a thirty-day rest period at home, as well as the money to get there!

Having been away for about 14 months, it was great to see the family, and quite a few friends living in Fernandina. Those 30 days really flew by. Before leaving, I told my parents that no one knew anything more than the fact that I would report to Ardmore, Oklahoma, for further training, probably in B-17's. The guessing was that most of the bomb crews would be heading for the European Theater of War. My Dad just shook his head and said to my mother, "I believe the government has lost their minds. They will be turning a brand new, half-a-million dollar airplane over to Jim and his crew members to fly across the Atlantic Ocean to Europe. I'm not sure he's mature enough to push a baby carriage around the block." I did make it to Ardmore, and ultimately navigated our crew across the North Atlantic to England!

A GREAT BUNCH – WE ALL SURVIVED! Back Row, L to R: Johnson – Navigator, McEwen – Co-Pilot, Hann – Pilot, Cooper – Bombardier. Front Row, L to R: Quagliano – Radio Operator, Simecek – Tail Gunner, Christmas – Flight Engineer, Morrison – Waist Gunner, Dersham – Ball Turret Gunner All of us were dressed for combat flight, where temperatures were about 60 degrees below zero. Oxygen masks above 10,000 feet completed our ensemble!

CHAPTER 2

THE B-17 & B-24 WORKHORSES OF WAR

DESTINATION: ENGLAND

Our crew assembled at Ardmore, Oklahoma, to become familiar with the B-17 Flying Fortress, and to begin the process of welding together all of us as a working team to prepare for combat conditions, prior to assignment for active duty overseas. Crew members broke down as follows:

Ray E. Hann – Pilot. *Previously served in the Army Infantry, probably about 24 at that time, Ray was hard as a rock from his prior military training, tall and thin, recently graduated from Air Force flight training, and well prepared for what laid ahead. He was "One of the Boys" on the ground, but in the air his decisions were final, and everyone understood that. A good man for the job.*

Pat McEwen – Co-Pilot. *Pat was a rather laid back individual, and a kind, genial fellow, somewhat on the quiet side. He lived in central Georgia, where I guess he was born, and evidently had been engaged in farming prior to his induction into the military, followed by Air Force flight training. We were fortunate to have him as part of the crew.*

Douglas M. Cooper – Bombardier. *Short and stocky, always with a smile on his face, Doug lived in California, where I presume he was raised, as that has been his home since the end of the war. Upon indoctrination into the service, he had followed the same path as*

others – basic training, being accepted for Bombardier training, and graduated. Now he was assigned to this particular crew, and was a great addition for our team.

Michael Quagliano – Radio operator and gunner. In 1943, he was drafted and assigned to the Army Air Corps. He was about 19 when we all met, tall and gangly, very outgoing, and loved to eat – particularly anything associated with his Italian background. Mike was raised as a devout Catholic boy, which may have had some bearing on his interest in radio. He also had another calling in communications – his Rosary Beads were always present, and when things really got rough on many of our missions, Hann would get on the interphone and say "Mike, we're in trouble – better get out your beads and get us some help from above!" We had a wonderful radio operator.

Milo Simecek – Tail Gunner. A big man to be in this cramped area of the tail position, but he got there and did a great job. He was married prior to becoming a part of the Air Force, and we all were patting him on the back over the arrival of a new daughter while overseas. Milo was quiet and didn't socialize much, but a good man to have in the crew.

Frances Christmas – Flight Engineer and Top Turret Gunner. Chris was a great engineer, capable of handling any emergency while airborne. He was rather short and slim as a reed, which permitted him to squeeze into a lot of small spaces if required. He flew with us for essentially all of our missions, returned to the states, and later participated in

the "Berlin Air Lift" carrying food, fuel, etc. to the Germans behind the "Berlin Wall." He was a very interesting person whom we all enjoyed seeing at 490th Bomb Group reunions in later years.

Jim Morrison – Waist Gunner. He was several years older than some of us, perhaps closer to Hann's age of 24. Jim was a fine fellow, always ready to help, jovial and friendly. He flew quite a few missions, but ultimately the stress and strain of combat got him – referred to as "flak happy," which caused him to be grounded and returned to the States. He was a good crew member and a fine fellow. He died sometime after the war in his New England home site.

Arthur Dersham – Ball Turret Gunner. Dersham had to be small in stature to fit into the ball turret, but he stood tall in all other respects. He hailed from Ann Arbor, Michigan, where he still resides with his wife and several children. After the war, he operated a pet shop business, which apparently prospered.

And then there was me, **E.J. Johnson, Jr.**, navigator.

Together, we formed Hann's crew of the 490th Bomb Group, a group now under the respected command of noneother than Frank Bostrom. We were truly a great gang, but we never thought that we would survive to see the 1980's or 1990's. Our survival and overall success as a unit can be directly attributed to the discipline and unwavering leadership provided by Bostrom.

As we started flying, everyone began to get the feel of the part they played. Each person became acclimated to the plane. I was delighted to be on the B-17 rather than the B-24, although both are workhorses in combat situations. The primary difference between the two planes was the design of each, particularly the wing configuration.

The B-24 fuselage was essentially suspended below the wing, which was built into the upper part of the body. The landing gear was fitted into a well on the bottom of the wing and was raised or lowered for takeoffs and landings by hydraulic action. When lowered, the bottom of the fuselage was actually elevated above the runway for clearance to function properly. This design worked beautifully for all normal flying, but in combat situations, planes suffered from a lot of unforeseen problems. Planes would lose engines, oil supply and radio transmission. Malfunctions would wipe out hydraulic lines that controlled the landing gear. When the landing gear was out and a B-24 had to make a crash landing, the fuselage took the full brunt of the impact. Because this design flaw led to many casualties, the B-24 became known in many circles as "The Flying Coffin." Despite all this, many B-24 crews felt they were perhaps the finest bombers in the air.

The B-17 configuration was completely different. On this plane, the wing was built into the bottom of the fuselage, which provided more lift. Like the B-24, the landing gear fit into the well below the wing, but the landing mechanism was much shorter than that

B-24 Bomber – Note the high wing placement and elevated tail. This plane and the B-17 below are owned & operated by the Collings Foundation for displays throughout the United States.

of the B-24 because of the wing location. Because of this, if a B-17 had to make a crash landing without its landing gear, both the wing and the fuselage shared the contact with the ground. Many B-17's, such as the renowned "Memphis Bell," looked as if there was no way to keep them flying, although they stayed in the air. All of these things made me thankful I had the good luck to be assigned to a B-17!

As wonderful as these bombers were, they had no insulation anywhere in the plane. The exterior sheet metal was attached to the framework of the plane and there was no way to include heat for subfreezing temperatures at flight altitudes; layers of clothing had to suffice. At high altitudes, anyone who touched metal without fleece lined gloves was in trouble – the skin would instantly freeze to the metal. Neither were there any "Comfort Facilities"... several relief tubes were a part of the equipment, but it didn't compare with today's aircraft!

Our days at Ardmore seemed to pass rather quickly, and we found ourselves spending a short time at home with family and friends before reporting to another base location for more duty.

Our next base location was Lincoln, Nebraska. This came as a surprise to me since we all knew that was where many crews departed for overseas duty. This meant aerial combat. My concern was that when my class graduated from Navigation School at Hondo, Texas, I had never had any training in gunnery school. This, I understood, would be worked into my schedule at a later date. Soon, word leaked around that we would be heading to the European Theater. For someone who didn't know anything about a 50-caliber machine gun, I learned quickly how to use it when someone was trying to shoot you down!

B-17 "Flying Fortress" – lower wing is clearly visible. These pictures taken during exhibits at Fernandina Beach and Jacksonville, Florida. These are probably the only two still flying – 1992.

Although we did not know what our destination would be, we began to prepare for our flight. We spent a lot of time looking over our new B-17G bomber, which had been assigned to us for ferrying to the war zone. In the course of becoming familiar with the plane, someone found the camera well in the belly of the fuselage, complete with a high altitude camera to take pictures of results from bombing missions. Since we were going to be flying across the Atlantic and had no bombs, we certainly didn't anticipate taking pictures. Because of this, someone decided that this equipment was not really needed for our trip. The camera was quietly removed, placed in a safe location at the air base, and this space was used for other purposes: The crew pooled their financial resources and invested in some Bourbon Whiskey. It was never known exactly who engineered this modification, but everyone approved it.

After departing from Lincoln, we flew to an air base at Grenier, New Hampshire, for an overnight stop. We checked and refueled the plane before heading to Goose Bay, Labrador. This part of the trip was filled with beautiful scenery as we flew across Canada. It was the late summer/early fall season: the snow had not arrived, the air was clear and every tree stood out in splendor. There were many lakes interspersed along the way, glimmering in the sunlight. It was an enjoyable flight.

SECRET
AUTH: CO GF
8-15-44

OPERATIONS ORDERS)
No......... 14)

E X T R A C T

/L/

15 August 1944

** ** ** ** ** **

7. The following named crews WP by air in the aircraft as indicated below at the proper time from Grenier Field, Manchester, New Hampshire, via North Atlantic Route to the European Theatre of Operations, London, England, reporting upon arrival thereat to the Commander, 8th Air Force Service Command, Air Transport Command Terminals of Arrival, British Isles, for further assignment and duty with the 8th Air Force.

Shipment No. FD- AJ-22 Project No. 92805-R APO No. 16403-AJ-22
   B-17G   Crew No. FD- AJ-22   #43-38351

2nd Lt.	WALTER, GEORGE F.
2nd Lt.	WOOD, ROBERT H.
2nd Lt.	FITZSIMMONS, JAMES J.
F/O	IANIUS, WALTER M., JR.
Cpl.	Hardin, Louis D.
Cpl.	Thwaite, James E.
Cpl.	Stojkov, Steven W.
Cpl.	Rhodes, Melvin A.
Cpl.	Richards, Edward P.
Cpl.	Parker, Barney, Jr.

Shipment No. FP- AA-167 Project No.
   B-24J   Crew No. FP-

2nd Lt.	CHRISTENSEN, CLARENCE, JR.
2nd Lt.	KASPAR, PAUL J.
2nd Lt.	LIVESAY, HAROLD A.
2nd Lt.	VAN ROOY, RUSSELL W.
Cpl.	Rischling, Kenneth E.
Cpl.	Huber, Charles H.
Cpl.	Taylor, Everett E.
Sgt.	Adkins, Charles C.
Cpl.	Lazzari, Bernard J.
Cpl.	Huey, Robert C.

Shipment No. FD- AJ-70 Project No. 92805-R APO No. 16403-AJ-70
   B-17G   Crew No. FD- AJ-70   #44-8270

2nd Lt.	HANN, RAY E., JR.	01301994	(P)
2nd Lt.	MC EWEN, PAT	0764919	(CP)
2nd Lt.	JOHNSON, EMANUEL J., JR.	0723628	(N)
2nd Lt.	COOPER, DOUGLAS M.	0776877	(B)
Cpl.	Christmas, Francis N.	32676534	(EG)
Cpl.	Quagliano, Michael C.	36669064	(ROG)
Sgt.	Morrison, James J.	11041870	(AG)
Cpl.	Dersham, Arthur C., Jr.	36419911	(CG)
Cpl.	Martin, Claude A.	38537588	(CG)
Cpl.	Simpcek, Milas	36893871	(CG)

-1-
SECRET

Copy of orders for our transfer to England & routing information. Note the "Secret" at top of document. Three crews covered to fly across North Atlantic route. Two B-17's & one B-24. Our crew, in skeleton size, with other fighter pilots, returned by the same route in 1945 after VE Day.

CHAPTER 3

PERILS OF FLYING TO ENGLAND
BY THE NORTH ATLANTIC ROUTE

When we arrived at Goose Bay, we found the sun still shining, even though everything farther south was, by then, blanketed in the darkness of night. It was good to have this part of our journey behind us. We were glad to get a solid meal at dinner, and we rested in preparation for our Atlantic crossing.

Our briefing the next morning was a procedure every crew passing through Goose Bay had to attend. The perils involved in successfully conquering the North Atlantic Route were unbelievable, with most of the stress and pressure resting squarely on the shoulders of the pilot and navigator. At age 20, I had just completed training at navigation school, and I had very limited knowledge of how to deal with the circumstances that lay ahead. It was an awesome situation. Most anything could happen in a short length of time. Decisions had to be made immediately and they had to be the right decisions: mistakes could lead to terrible consequences, including crash landings in the ocean. These realizations scared me to death.

Weather was always unsettled and sudden violent changes occurred. Forecast prediction was a crapshoot. Ice and snow, intense rains, heavy cloud cover and headwinds that caused excessive drains on fuel were just a few of the circumstances we encountered.

When leaving Goose Bay, the distance to Iceland was approximately 1,500 miles. If any problems developed prior to reaching that point, the only option for landing was Greenland. The entrance to the small airport facilities was scarred with ragged mountains and narrow canyons covered with snow and ice.

The B-17 had a fuel capacity of 2,800 gallons, and those 4 huge engines gulped down the gas. Preservation of every ounce of fuel was important. Even when crews successfully reached Iceland, sometimes the inclement weather prevented landings. This was called a "point of no return." Getting back to Goose Bay was an impossibility since there was insufficient fuel for a trip to Canada. The other alternative was to fly an additional 800 miles to the ultimate destination, an air base in Wales. Many planes, each with 9 crew members aboard, were lost along the way.

After our briefing cautioned us on all these hazards and provided us with information concerning false radio signals from German U-boats, Norway, and other interference, we went to the flight line to prepare for take-off. The weather was terrible. Dense cloud cover was almost to ground level, rain was coming down in sheets and heavy winds were blowing in from Greenland. This meant we would be fighting head winds, causing excess fuel consumption – not a good omen. Nonetheless, we were ready for our journey.

After receiving clearance from the control tower, we moved into the take-off position on the runway. With a lot of prayers and fingers crossed, we rolled down the strip, gathering speed for lift-off. Once airborne, we climbed through heavy rain to reach flight altitude, where, to our horror, we saw that a fuel cap for one of the gas tanks in the wing was missing and gas was spewing out in the wind. There was no option – we turned around and headed back to the Goose Bay air base. Upon arrival, the gas tanks were all "topped off" and checks were made to be certain that every tank was properly sealed. Once again, under very bad weather conditions, we took off for Iceland.

Arriving at the flight altitude of 5,000 feet, we passed over the southern tip of Greenland, where we saw the rocky terrain of ice- and snow-covered mountains, as well as massive icebergs floating in the sea. To our astonishment, we also had blue flames dancing along the leading edge of our wing. In the middle of the Atlantic, we didn't want to see anything that looked like fire. All hands checked everything possible, found no problems aboard the plane, and finally concluded we were looking at St. Elmo's Fire – the same freak occurrence reported by ancient mariners crossing the sea.

Reykjavik, Iceland, was 800 miles away, and while we hoped weather conditions would permit us to land, every effort was made to conserve gas, just in case. After what seemed like a very long time, we were near enough to have radio contact with the airport at Reykjavik. To our great relief, we received word that weather conditions permitted us to land.

Reykjavik greeted us with cold, barren terrain. No trees were visible in the immediate area, and only a few houses were scattered around the base. They housed us in Quonset huts. There was a small town several miles away, but we were too beat to have any desire for sightseeing. All we had wanted was to arrive safely, and now our minds were focused on getting something to eat and resting. Touching down in Iceland, we were thankful that we could put enough gas in the tanks to assure our arrival at the air base in Wales.

After a night's rest, we prepared for the final leg of our trip. After a stop at the mess hall for breakfast, we were briefed at the flight line. Our briefing included weather reports and radio signals for our flight path. With this information in hand, we went to our plane, where a very complete inspection was made. Orders from flight control moved us into position for take-off, and we headed southeast toward Wales after climbing to altitude.

ICELAND ACCOMMODATIONS *Pat McEwen standing in front of the "Iceland Ritz." Note the obviously barren conditions there.*

The 800-mile route took about six hours, but after the 1500-mile flight to Iceland, the trip to Wales was a piece of cake. Radio contact with the control tower in Wales gave us the flight pattern for landing, so we landed without incident in England. All of our belongings were removed from the plane, which was then officially turned over to the 8th Air Force. One more B-17 had arrived for war in the European Theater.

After an overnight stay there, we were transferred to London. Our stay there for a couple of days gave us time to see the damage inflicted by the Germans. It was a very strange situation to anyone who had never seen the place. Magnificent buildings constructed centuries ago suffered extensive damage. Many bulidings had whole sections destroyed and black soot from fires was everywhere. Rubble was being cleared from the streets while major repairs were underway to return streets to a usable condition. It was utter chaos.

In the midst of all this, the British people were dealing with the situation in a very calm manner. Since gasoline was required for military activities, propane gas was used as fuel for vehicles. Every taxi had a huge collapsible tank on top of the roof, which depleted as the gas was consumed (a sure-fire way to know when to get more petrol). When darkness fell, all lights were either cut off or shaded in some way. London was a city of darkness...anything to make it that much more difficult for the Germans to destroy.

This was also my first introduction to

"Buzz Bombs," self-propelled missiles launched from sites across the English Channel and the North Sea. These inflicted much of the damage in the area. The engines were very audible as the bombs passed overhead. Everyone in the area knew that so long as you could hear the "putt, putt, putt" of the engine, it was safe to assume the intended target was beyond your location. Everyone also knew, however, that if the noise suddenly stopped, it was best to either dive for the closest ditch or get into a bomb shelter.

CHAPTER 4

ELEMENTS OF WAR

U ntil you have been involved in fighting a war, you can never fully understand the circumstances of combat. Though many confrontations have occured throughout history, few equal the magnitude of World War II.

Hitler controlled Germany, but sought to conquer all of Europe and Asia, and eventually the world. Toward this end, he annexed France, Belgium, Austria and most of the other smaller European countries. After working out an alliance with Mussolini for control of Italy, the tempo of combat increased. During this

The scene in the Reichstag as Hitler announced to the German nation that Germany was at war with the United States. December 11, 1941.

reign of oppression, things got very nasty. Literally millions of Jews, and any other groups who opposed Hitler, were rounded up in concentration camps and brutally murdered. There were still hundreds of thousands of servicemen who had been killed in combat. It was simply a devastating period of history.

For those indoctrinated into war, the first lesson learned is kill or be killed. If you see the enemy and do not kill him, he will kill you. Another lesson quickly learned is that one must strike with great force. The more power used in the initial strike, the greater one's chances are of winning. This applies to personnel, planes and land combat equipment (such as armored tanks and trucks).

Another dominant consideration is the element of surprise. This was executed by the Japanese in the sneak attack on Pearl Harbor on December 7, 1941. Thousands of our personnel were killed, and the majority of aircraft carriers, battleships and cruisers assigned to the Pacific area were sunk, burned or otherwise destroyed. Military airfields, bases and storage facilities in the Pearl Harbor/Manila vicinity were destroyed, and our defenses, as a nation, were essentially wiped out in one tragic attack by this enemy. As unbelievable as it may seem, reports indicate that President Franklin D. Roosevelt was alerted prior to this attack that large numbers of Japanese fleets of ships were moving toward the Philippine Islands, but the commanding officers at Pearl Harbor and Manila were not advised of potential danger.

With the United States military flat on

their backs, Hitler pressed harder for control of England, Russia and other areas of Europe while Japan expanded its efforts to control the Pacific area. With the attack coming at the U.S. from both sides, it is remarkable that we were able to produce planes, ships and military vehicles to hold off the two enemies at the same time. Had it not been for the spirit of the American people, this country would not have survived. The magnitude of Japan's sneak attack on Pearl Harbor galvanized the entire country. People looked at it as a personal matter, so everyone took part in trying to regain the dignity and honor for which the U.S. had long been recognized.

Women rushed to perform jobs normally held by men so the men could go fight the war. Most of the women had to get fast training and were employed as steel workers, riveters and mechanics. They rapidly became efficient enough to build thousands of army tanks, trucks, airplanes and ocean-going ships, earning the nickname "Rosie the Riveter." In addition to working in domestic factories, women volunteered for work in hospitals and in the Red Cross. Along with nursing, women also drove trucks and other emergency vehicles.

Young men were conscripted for military service in large numbers, but hundreds of thousands also enlisted to contribute their efforts before reaching draft age. That generation fought and died for the honor and preservation of our constitutional freedoms. Unfortunately, generations of this era have little knowledge of WWII circumstances 55 years ago. It was an age when our character was defined by victory in that war. Yes, things are different today...and our outlooks today are shaped by the dynamics of our current culture, but we need to do everything within our power to prevent future wars. It would probably be difficult to meet the challenges of that bygone era.

CHAPTER 5

THE 8TH AIR FORCE

The command groups sent to England to set up the 8th Air Force were all outstanding men whose names were legendary. General "Hap" Arnold was responsible for the overall structure of this armada and how it would function. General Carl "Tooey" Spaatz was put in charge of the first units to arrive in England. General James H. Doolittle (famed for his raid on Japan after their attack on Pearl Harbor), General Ira Eaker and General Curtis E. Lemay were all involved in the daylight bombing activities for which the 8th was famous.

The Mighty Eighth was so named because it had 200,000 persons actively engaged by June of 1944, and 350,000 men were estimated to have served during the time the 8th was active. The Stars and Stripes Newspaper for the armed services in the European Theater carried a front page picture of more than 1,000 bombers from the Mighty Eighth dropping 2,500 tons of bombs on Berlin in a raid February 3, 1945. The Stars and Stripes reported that this armada of aircraft stretched almost 300 miles across the continent. These startling statistics are almost beyond comprehension when one considers the amount of personnel, bombers, fighters and ground support activities involved.

Airfields had to be constructed to provide bases of operations as close as possible to the

European target areas. This meant the section of England known as East Anglia was the spot. East Anglia covered an area approximately 40 miles wide and 80 miles long on the northeast side of London. It was a section of beautiful estates and large farming activities during peacetime, but this was not peactime and the allies were fighting for survival. The English Government took over the entire area with the understanding that the land would be returned to the owners after cessation of the war. In East Anglia, which was approximately the size of Vermont, at least 130 airfields were reported to have been built. These included bases for B-17 and B-24 bombers, our P-47 and P-51 fighters, as well as some of England's own defense operations. Through necessity, the airfields were all very close to each other: many were separated by only about five miles. This greatly increased the danger of mid-air collisions.

When the United States and England became in aerial warfare with the Germans, the U.S. began constructing many thousands of bombers for transfer to England. Obviously there had to be bases for these planes to operate from, as well as many other changes for coordination of necessary wartime functions. The English people were very ingenious in developing these facilities. The rubble from the German bombings on London and other cities had to be removed, so they loaded this into railroad cars for shipment to designated areas and used the bricks, concrete, and rubble as a base for runways to build the airfields.

All of the approximately 130 airfields had three runways for take-off and landing. Essentially the same pattern of design applied to all of the bases, with taxi strips surrounding the perimeter for access to and from the runways. Scattered around the taxi strips were the concrete areas for parking the bombers, known as hard stands. Each hard stand could accommodate several planes, and these areas were purposefully scattered out to minimize loss in case of German attacks. For additional protection, these areas usually had some type of revetment around them.

Arrival of the 8th Air Force in England introduced daylight bombing. The English flew their bombing sorties at night, so there was no conflict between the two allies' missions. With this arrangement, bombs could be rained on German targets nearly 24 hours a day, and since each of the two air commands had their own bases, all repair work and pre-flight checks could be properly carried out.

Daylight bombing meant that German fighter planes could see our bombers 40 to 50 miles away at altitudes of 25,000 to 28,000 feet. Their mission was to attack and shoot down every one possible on the way to the targets, or to catch stragglers who suffered damage over the target and could not maintain a position within the bomb group. The German fighters would not attack once the bomb run commenced and bomb bay doors were open because the intense flak from ground forces shooting anti-aircraft artillery could also knock down their own fighters. There was usually a lot of turbulence on the bomb runs. The turbulence could flip a plane around like a leaf in a storm. This encouraged us to loosen the formation a little until we were over the target and dropped our bomb loads. Leaving the target, the ranks were closed so the firepower of our collective 50-caliber machine guns could offer greater protection, and so there were no holes in the bomb train for enemy fighters to streak through with machine guns blazing. The trip "home" could be even more scary than going to the target, particularly if some damage had been sustained over the bomb run, a common occurence. The loss of an engine, damage to any of the plane control surfaces such as rudders, flaps, landing gear or bomb bay doors were all dominant factors in being able to keep up with other planes in the bomb train. Should it become impossible to do so, your chances of survival diminished greatly, and the German fighters could spot the debilitated planes immediately as a prime target.

Perhaps the most intriguing question was how to get 1,000 bombers airborne and assembled into a bomb train with bad weather and low visibilty until 15,000 feet. All the planes from bases as close as 5 miles... all trying to accomplish the same thing at the same time. The solution to this problem was a "laddering" climb to altitude to assemble above the cloud cover. At the pre-flight briefings, and with radio communications from the flight control center, the headings and the rate of climb were all confirmed and verified. Assuming that the headings for climbing the ladder were due North and due South, as soon as the wheels left the runway, the North heading would be established. The rate of climb kicked in, and that heading was maintained for 5 minutes. At that point, a turn was made to due South heading (180 degrees), the same rate of climb was kept, and for 5 minutes this heading was maintained, followed by another turn back to due North. These procedures continued until the plane reached the level where skies were clear, and the assembly process got underway.

This "ladder" led to very close calls, as well as some mid-air collisions. Ray Hann referred to these problems in his diary: *"All of us 'sweated out' a takeoff with a full load of gasoline and bombs. Many planes exploded before they had gotten two miles. Bad visibility, ice on the wings and the runways caused most of this. We assembled anywhere between 6,000 to 25,000 ft., going up through overcast, often as much as 15,000 ft. thick, - planes would collide and never know what hit them. It wasn't unusual to find ourselves in propwash, and never see the other plane. The assembly itself was tricky, with a heavy plane and a whole division in one area, they often collided."*

Even after taking-off and achieving position in the bomb train, some malfunctions could occur – fuel leaks, loss of oil, pressure leaks in hydraulic systems or radio problems could develop. In the event of unexpected complications, the pilot was responsible for deciding whether to abort or to continue the mission. To abort was really a last resort, since the bombs would have to be dropped into the North Sea, tremendous amounts of fuel were wasted, and getting back to the base through heavy cloud cover was very dangerous to deal with. After going through all the flight preliminaries such as waking at 2:00 AM, swallowing breakfast, attending briefings and checking out the plane on the flight line, nearly 4 hours were spent preparing for the mission. So it was never an easy decision whether to continue a crippled plane or to abort, but on a flight of 2,000 miles to target and return, trying to fly on three engines instead of four would have meant almost certain death. Every bomber had four huge engines, which were required to lift the plane's 35 tons off the ground and to travel long distances at high altitudes. Each one had propellers with three blades mounted on a heavy steel shaft, which have an arc of about 12 feet. The turbulence generated by all 4 of these engines at maximum operating levels created a very bumpy and tricky environment for planes behind them.

Even when all went well and the plane did not malfunctrion, crews faced other hardships while in mid-air. Temperatures at our flight altitudes of 25,000 to 28,000 feet usually registered about 60 degrees below zero. Bombers had no insulation for protection against these death-dealing elements of nature, so the only alternative was clothing. Our outfits consisted of "Long John" underwear, heavy woolen shirts and trousers and an electric suit, which was similar to today's electric blanket. The jacket and trousers were equipped with small electrical wiring, which tied into the primary cord from an electrical source. Very similar to today's cigarette lighter in automobiles, the primary cord was plugged into the plane's electrical system and a thermostat controlled the temperature. Over these layers, we wore fleece-lined leather jackets, pants, boots, helmets and gloves to protect from frostbite.

In maximum effort missions (1,000 plus planes, making a bomb train about 300 miles long) 4,000 props would churn up the air en route to targets. Such extreme turbulence could throw planes around like leaves in a hurricane. It was not uncommon to be flying straight and level and then suddenly drop 2,000 feet. Flying in close formation for greatest protection from Nazi fighters, these sudden drops often caused mid-air collisions.

Weather was another vital factor. The British Isles have the most unpredictable weather conditions imaginable. North Atlantic weather conditions change frequently, and fog, intense cloud coverage, rain, snow or wild winds could occur spontaneously. The 8th Air Force had probably the best forecasters of WWII; however, their predictions were rarely accurate. Obviously, bombing raids were vital to the protection of our ground forces involved in combat, but the weather controlled the ability of our bomb groups to fly.

When Air Force Headquarters selected targets for the bombers and weather conditions appeared to be favorable for flight, the groups selected for the missions were advised to be on "stand-by alert." The group commanders then determined which crews should fly, and those selected would need to "hit the sack" for as much rest as possible. At some awful hour, often between 2:00 a.m. and 4:00 a.m., a flashlight in the face would suddenly awaken the chosen crews, and the directions were clear: "You're flying – briefing will be in one hour and forty-five minutes from now." This meant the crews had to get up immediately. Shaving was mandatory because oxygen masks were required at any altitude above 10,000 feet and the masks did not fit properly over whiskers. Soldiers then made a beeline for the mess hall and breakfast. Crews knew they must eat very heartily, since the next meal would likely be no earlier than 7:00 p.m. — that is if you weren't shot down along the way to or from the target. From there, it was the flight line and briefing.

The briefing was a complete disclosure of planned routes, details for takeoffs, information on the areas of ground artillery shelling, length of today's mission, codes and anything else elemental to the day's mission. Everyone entering was checked by military personnel for security, and once inside a large blackboard was covered over until the Base Commander, or some designated individual, appeared to discuss mission details. The pilot, co-pilot, navigator, and bombardier attended this briefing. These sessions were always disturbing and scary. Everyone knew where the rough targets were, and if the mission that day was to be Berlin, Merseburg, or some other targets of 1,000 miles each way, the anxiety and fright was terrible. After the briefing, vehicles carried the crew to the hardstand where the plane was parked.

The ground crews had been working all night, checking engine performance, loading bombs and topping off gas tanks (usually to the maximum of 2,780 gallons of 100 octane fuel). The enlisted crew personnel, crew chief, radio operator, and gunners were busy checking the 50-caliber machine guns, the radio and intercom operations, comparing notes with the ground crew and generally assuring that the plane was ready for takeoff on time.

Flak was one of the most deadly enemies a flight crew could encounter. The Germans had mobile units of heavy artillery cannons at many strategic sites all over European areas under their control. These were used to defend their targets by shooting down U.S. and English bombers. The Germans used 88 mm shells, which were set to explode at our cruising altitude. The explosions sprayed chunks of metal in their target areas, which were points on our bombing runs. Flak could tear holes through the wings and debilitate engines, wipe out hydraulic functions and kill occupants in the planes. A direct hit could pulverize a bomber, leaving only small bits of metal and dust. It was very disturbing to see a plane directly in front of you vaporized.

The German strategy was to darken the sky with a "box" of flak at the level our planes were flying. With the bombers heading over the target with bomb doors open, this was a deadly situation. Many planes were shot down, and others who had suffered damage could not maintain position with the group and were prime targets for German fighters.

The main defense air crews had against the flak were Flak Jackets, which were really more of a blanket than a jacket. These were the granddaddy of bulletproof vests. Flak Jackets were essential on bomb runs to protect the vital parts of your body from flying particles. Constructed of a heavy material similar to canvas, it covered the front and rear of the body from shoulders to thighs, Small steel plates inside the material provided protection in much the same way that bulletproof vests do today. This unit weighed about 50 pounds, so you didn't want to carry it for long periods, but it was a wonderful protection to have in combat conditions.

Doug Cooper, our bombardier, had a position in the very front of plane's nose where he controlled the Norden Bombsight which directed the bomb drop. In that spot, surrounded by plexiglass, there was not much to provide protection from the flak. Fortunately, the bombs had been dropped already when a piece of flak about 2" x 4" ripped through the nose with enough velocity to knock Cooper out of his seat. As a bomb run precaution, all of the crew members were wearing their flak jackets, and because of that, the missle didn't penetrate Doug's flesh. However, my position was also in the nose (just behind the bombsight) so when Doug came hurtling backwards, he hit me full force and we were both lucky to not have any injuries. When we arrived back at our base, we noticed the fuselage had way too many holes to bother counting. It had been quite a day.

This Stars and Stripes photo shows two dramatic scenes-the liberation of Paris, where Nazi snipers shot many people, and the air drops of what appears to be hundreds of parachutes, putting our troops behind the German lines.

CHAPTER 6

WAR IS HELL

October 2, 1944 was indeed a memorable day. It was our first combat mission, and the target was in the Ruhr Valley of Germany. The area was a highly industrialized section which produced many items vital to the German war effort. Because of this, this area up and down the Rhine river was protected by one of the heaviest fortifications of anti-aircraft artillery.

The target for our particular group was a railroad marshalling yard where trains were shifted around in the process of delivering troops and materials of war to their respective destinations. Our mission was to bomb the rail facilities to prevent these weapons from getting to their destination. Our pre-flight briefing had advised all the crews that we would encounter heavy flak within the area and over the target. This being our first mission to experience aerial warfare, we didn't really know exactly what to expect.

Approaching the target, the sky was black from 88mm shells exploding all around us. The bomb bay doors were open, the bombs were ready to be dropped and there was no alternative but to pray that we would survive the onslaught. As the bombs dropped, a large black puff of smoke exploded in front of us, and suddenly our number three engine was on fire. The pilot opened the engine cowlings, cut off the engine and dove about 1500 feet to extinguish the fire.

Fortunately, there were no enemy fighters in the area and we were able to climb back to the altitude of the troop heading back to merry 'ol England. We had taken some hits and had holes in the plane from the flak, but other than the loss of that one engine, we seemed to be okay. Heavy clouds over Europe were common, and on this day, as we dropped to lower altitudes, visibility was obscured and pretty intense buffeting of the plane was encountered. Any aircraft in this situation will probably experience up and down movement of the wing tips, perhaps three, four, or more feet, depending on the turbulence. The heavy cloud cover obscured visibility during the let down to a very low level over the English Channel when an ominous hole was spotted in the left wing. Blue flames were streaking out of the hole, but by this time, we were at an approximate altitude of 500 feet, and much too low to bail out since the parachutes wouldn't have time to fully deploy. We knew the plane could blow to smithereens at any second, but we were trapped. Our only chance for survival was to pray we could land before the explosion. Quagliano got out his rosary beads ... seeking divine assistance to get us down in one piece. Hann got away from other planes in the formation and called in a "mayday" distress signal for the group tower to clear the runways for us. The lower we got, the heavier the flames became until the whole wing was engulfed. The instant that the wheels touched concrete, Ray used brakes, flaps, and anything available to stop our forward movement.

Quagliano, Dersham, Morrison, and Simecek got out through the rear door, which was on the right side of the plane, and not in the line of fire from the wing on the left side. Hann, McEwen, Christmas, Cooper and I were still trapped since the props were "windmilling" enough to decapitate anyone who happened to get too close. It seemed an eternity before they stopped, and the five of us in the front could get out through the lower escape hatch under the nose. With our feet on terra firma, we all ran like scalded dogs and dove behind a mound of dirt. There we remained just waiting for the explosion... it never occurred.

This picture of Kassel, Germany, was taken from 28,000 feet. Our crew was hit over our target, which ignited fire in left wing. Art Dersham got this birds-eye shot from his ball turret position. October 2, 1944

This is the original picture of ground crews putting out the fire.

Ambulances, fire trucks and ground crews with foam and equipment to put out the fire arrived very quickly and began trying to save the plane. Though the fire was put out, the plane was destroyed and probably had little salvage value.

We later discovered the miraculousness of our experience. The circumstances indicated that a shell had gone through the wing and exploded above the plane. With the gas tanks in the wing, we could have had an explosion over the target or on our return to friendly territory. I have often wondered if the up and down movement of the wing may have caused damaged spars in the wing to rub against each other enough to ignite the fire, but no one knows. Despite the flak, fire and turbulence, no one was injured.

Pictures of the ground crew fighting the fire engulfing the plane were sent back to the States by Air Force Headquarters, where they appeared in every major paper as part of the effort to sell war bonds. The reprint of this report appeared in the New York Times. Public Relations in the 490th Bomb Group sent reports to hometowns of the crew members that stated we had "ridden a hot bomber for 600 miles."

This photo was used by the New York Times. Note "490" written at top to designate bomb group.

What a way to be indoctrinated to aerial combat missions! We were all glad to be greeted by the Red Cross girls bringing us drinks of bourbon, scotch and other spirits to settle our nerves.

Hann was later presented the Distinguished Flying Cross, a very outstanding award for his efforts and skill in getting the plane and crew on the ground with no casualties! We had an excellent pilot.

October 7, 1944
Merseburg

Our second mission found us assigned to bomb Merseburg, one of the toughest targets in the European Theater War Zone. Located in the far eastern section of Germany, this was probably the largest concentration of oil refining operations that fueled the Nazi war machine. Merseburg was far from bases in England and had a high concentration of anti-aircraft batteries in place, comparable to those surrounding Berlin.

After our first experience riding a hot bomber for 600 miles, the reports from other crews who had previously been to Merseburg caused most of our crew to be petrified. When you're about 20 years old, without a lot of previous experience to draw from, it's very easy to envision a drastic disaster over such a target. Having been assigned to the mission, our fate was sealed.

At the preflight briefing, we were warned of the artillery and flak, but no one was prepared for what we saw. Forty miles away from the target, the sky was black. German fighter planes were stationed along our route and we were encountering flak in areas where none was expected; it had already been a long, harrowing day, and we were not anywhere close to the target. As we reached the initial point (IP) of the bomb run and headed to the target, we saw something no fighter wants to see: for the first time, we saw a B-17 shot out of the sky. Hann wrote of the strange realities of the experience: *"Just as we came off the bomb run, a piece of shrapnel came up between Pat's legs* [Co-pilot McEwen]. *I could see his expression in spite of the oxygen mask. There was dirt and grime all over him. As serious as it was, I couldn't help but laugh. We picked up a few holes, nothing serious except #2 engine was hit and I had to feather the prop."*

Over the target anti-aircraft fire was intense, as could be seen from the huge black cloud over the entire area. Planes were dropping out of the sky above and below our altitude, like a swarm of flies. All the crew was on high alert to monitor these disasters, and keep Hann and McEwen aware of any potential mid-air collisions. Once the bombs were dropped Ray dove to lower levels to get out of the target zone, evaluate damages and check to see if any of the crew were injured. Hann seemed relieved to have come through the target zone in as good shape as we were, one engine out, and bullet holes in the fuselage, but no injuries. The rest of us still had major concerns about the 1000 mile trek back to England as Nazi fighter planes remained on the prowl for crippled aircraft such as ours.

We were scared to death, but managed to get back to England with only three engines. Henceforth, the word "Merseburg" left everyone in our group fearful of future missions to that target. At flight altitudes of about 28,000 feet, the temperature was around 60 degrees below zero. In spite of long johns, heavy clothing, fleece-lined pants, jacket, gloves, and helmets, it was still cold. However, in spite of that, very few crewmembers on these types of missions ever returned to base without shedding buckets of cold sweat!

October 1944 was a busy month for our crew and the 490th Bomb Group. After our first two missions to Kassel on the 2nd and the experience at Merseburg on the 7th, we thought enough had happened to make us seasoned veterans in aerial combat. We soon realized, however, that we still had a lot to learn.

October 19, 1944
Gustavsburg, Germany

Our records do not indicate what the target was, but the weather was terrible. There was very little flak, for which we were thankful, but it was impossible to see the ground, so the accuracy of our bombs was questionable. However, it is frustrating to go through all the preparations for a mission, check all of the pre-flight activities, fight the weather to reach the area above the clouds for assembly of the bomb train, reach the target for the bomb run, and when it's over, to have no satisfaction of knowing if the target was actually hit. However, you are thankful that the mission produced no great problems, which we called a "milk run."

October 15, 1944
Cologne, Germany
The target was a railroad marshalling yards to disrupt the transportation of men and materials. Unfortunately, there was heavy cloud cover from the time we left the French border, so the results of our bombing were questionable. We were at the end of the flight formation, so we had a very bumpy ride to and from the target. Fortunately, the flak was fairly light, we had no major mechanical problems and no one was hurt.

October 17, 1944
Cologne, Germany
Our target was again to hit the marshalling yards. The weather was the same as our experience two days earlier. However, there was a lot more flak over the target area this time, and we took a hit which caused the loss of our #2 engine. The oil pressure dropped, presumably from a broken fuel line, which may have been the result of flak – no one really knows. Hann feathered the prop, so we headed back to England with 3 engines. Fortunately, there was no severe damage from a mechanical standpoint, and the crew was intact. We did manage to limp back to our base, thankfully.

October 25, 1944
Hamburg, Germany
Hamburg, located in the northernmost

WELCOME TO THE TARGET FOR TODAY!

Just enough "flak" for German troops to let you know they have your exact altitude – note bomb bay door open & ready for drop. In this situation, there is no way to take evasive action.

Bombs Away! Pilot takes back control of plane from the bombardier, doors are closed, plane dives for greater speed, and to get out of flak – crew checked for any injuries or damage. Hoping to avoid German fighter planes waiting to shoot down bombers.

A full load of bombs dropped and on way to target. There are 12 bombs, and each weighs 500 pounds. Center of picture shows bombs exploding on impact. This may have been a railroad yard.

B-17's flying through a field of flak

part of Germany near the border of Denmark and adjacent to the North Sea, was a large port with a lot of ship traffic and many industrial activities. Because of the importance of these operations to maritime activities, there was a heavy concentration of anti-aircraft artillery to protect it from allied bombings. Our target was an oil refinery.

On that day, cloud cover was very heavy and visual on the refinery was poor. While we did not have adequate visual confirmation as to the target's location, we were in the bomb train close to the lead ship. Our bomb drop was as scheduled from the leader and considering the weather with the smoke rising into the clouds, it appeared that we did make a direct hit on the refinery. Afterwards, we counted 56 separate holes in the fuselage from anti-aircraft flak which gave us some very scary feelings realizing how close we came to serious injuries or death.

October 30, 1944
Merseburg

Hann felt the same as the rest of the crew; he did not want to return to this target which had given us so much trouble before: *"I sure wish we would hit this place once and for all"*

As was true on our previous missions to Merseburg, we encountered a phenomenal amount of flak on the October 7, 1944 mission. We were told that additional anti-aircraft artillery had indeed been added and that the protection in Merseburg had surpassed that surrounding Berlin. The sky was black, and the German's anti-aircraft accuracy was deadly. The Germans were intent on protecting this facility at any cost, but the recent intensity of allied bombing sent them a clear message we were equally intent on destroying the complex. One of the B-17's from the 848th Squadron of the 490th Bomb Group was lost. My own recollection is that so many planes were out of control, all crew members were looking out above and on each side to let the pilot know if evasive action was required to avoid mid-air collisions. The damage to so many planes led Hann to conclude that for those who survived, it would take more than several days just to put the planes in useable condition. After dropping the bombs, we headed out of the target zone and out of the flak area to reassemble enough planes to begin trying to head for England. It was a real nasty mess, and anyone who lived through it was lucky.

November 6, 1944
Neumunster, Germany

The six-day gap between our last mission

and this one provided enough time to repair and replace planes that were destroyed. This brought us back to an operational level. Neumunster was just north of Hamburg, so we knew there were many anti-aircraft weapons in the area. Our mission this time was to bomb railroad marshalling yards. We encountered moderate flak on the bomb run, but after dropping our twelve 500-pound "calling cards," we encountered very heavy and accurate flak in areas where it was not expected. Our crew was flying "Deputy Lead" plane for the mission that day and received instructions from the Group Leader to "scatter". Hann's records show the following comments – *"I dove a couple of thousand feet and turned first right and then to the left. I couldn't believe it when I saw one of my wingmen still with me. We regrouped and headed home."* It was a long trip over the North Sea before getting back to our base, but we made it, rejoicing that we had no casualties and delighted to have one more mission now behind us.

November 9, 1944
Saarbrucken, Germany

Located just south of Luxemburg, it was not too far from the Swiss border, so this was a long mission. As usual, the weather was terrible for flying, but we finally got to the "Initial Point" of the bomb run. (The IP was the starting point, selected to take advantage of jet stream winds behind the planes, which did increase our speed to get out of the target area as fast as possible.) Hann's diary is quoted herewith – *"We had to drop our payload on signal from the lead plane. They were using something called "Radar". The weather was so bad we had to separate and come back on our own. At one point, the lightning was so fierce that we had to turn the lights on in the cockpit to keep it from blinding us. A lightning bolt hit our left wing and rolled across the right wing."* Obviously, this was a terrible trek back to England, with awful weather conditions, essentially no visibility, many other planes in the same circumstances, floundering around at different elevations, and very little in the way of navigational tools to rely on for proper headings, etc. We ultimately got back to the area of our base, and again, Hann's comments are being quoted – *"When we finally were able to land, we had to approach the runway through cloud and fog until we could see it. We came over at 1,500 feet to get the proper direction, then did a tight 360 degree turn letting down until we wound up on the runway. That's bad enough, but a British Lancaster bomber loomed into sight at our altitude. I swear I could see the pilot we were so close. Fortunately, he pulled up, and I went down. We landed, but I must have bounced in like a basketball."* This was a very rough mission, and the entire crew was pretty badly shaken but, we managed to get back and survive! One more under our belts, and by now, we all considered ourselves to be seasoned veterans of combat. Our luck was continuing!

November 16, 1944
Duren, Germany

The weather was so terrible, we were told

at our briefing session that our base would most likely be "socked in" when the mission would be completed, so the alternate landing area would be at a place named Lille, France. After take off, climbing to the assembly altitude, and taking our position in the bomb train, we headed toward the English Channel en route to the target. Over the Channel, #2 engine lost oil pressure, so Hann had to feather the prop, abort the mission, dump our bomb load into the Channel, and return to England. His diary covers the situation which we encountered – *"We could not land at our base and were diverted to Carnaby, a British air base. They too were heavily socked in, but there was a huge bubble in the cloud cover. We had to fly into the cloud and let down at a certain rate. After about 4,000 feet, flying absolutely blind, we broke out at an elevation about 200 feet. The runway looked like a Christmas garden with tiny lights along each side. Actually, they had 50-gallon drums full of oil flaming. The heat from the drums is what caused the bubble in the cloud."* Ingenious people, our British friends, thinking of such a unique way to get planes down for landing despite the weather. We were glad to find a place to land that plane, but unfortunately, after all preparations for the mission, our efforts didn't count since we had to abort the mission.

November 21, 1944
Railroad bridge at Lingen, Germany

In reviewing the missions completed, the railroads and related activities have been important targets, due to their contribution in moving men and materials to oppose our efforts both on the ground and in the air. On this trip, we did not encounter a lot of resistance, perhaps in part due to the very heavy cloud cover in that area. Two of our planes collided and went down. We didn't know the crews, as all of us had a tendency not to become too close to the other crews, even those living in the same Quonset hut. One day, they're roommates, but the next day, they've been shot down in action over Germany and suddenly, you find yourself cleaning out their personal belongings to ship back to their families. You make space so some other new crew can have a place to stay. This had happened to us twice by this date, and it was very depressing. It would have been worse if all individuals in the hut had become very close friends.

November 22, 1944
Test Flight

It wasn't a mission, but this day qualified as one of our most unbelievable experiences of the war. Our entire crew was gathered together in our Quonset hut, otherwise known as "home," when Major Adams, our squadron commander, came in unexpectedly. He requested us to test fly one of the B-17's which had sustained severe damage on a previous mission. The Major wanted us to make sure everything was okay so the aircraft could return to combat duty. Hann agreed and we gathered a minimum crew, consisting of McEwen, myself, Christmas, and Quagliano.

Morrison, one of the gunners on the crew, wanted to go along for the ride, so the six of us headed for the flight line to prepare for take-off.

For those who can't remember, or don't know about the era of the 1940's, anyone who bought a new car then was admonished by the dealer to drive the first 500 to 1,000 miles at speeds of 40 to 50 miles per hour, before accelerating to highway speeds. This was called a "breaking in period" for the engine. The same principle applied to aircraft engines, and was called "slow time flying."

The plane we were testing had some engines replaced, new gas tanks installed in the right wing, plus other necessary repairs. We took off, one of the few days when we could actually see the sky, and at a time when mission flights had long been gone, so we had the whole sky to play around in, darting around clouds, etc. After the required time of several hours, we returned to our base for landing. As we approached the runway for landing, Hann "chopped" the throttle to reduce air speed for touch down, and this caused an "arc" or "backfire" from one of the engines on the right wing. When this occurred, the right wing burst into a sheet of solid flames while we were still traveling at a speed of perhaps 90 miles per hour. Quagliano and Morrison were in the rear part of the plane, terrified at what they were seeing. One of them pulled the pin to release the entrance / exit door from the fuselage so they could bail out before the expected explosion occurred. Quagliano got there first, but he froze.

Morrison kicked him out of the plane, then jumped right behind him.

Those of us in the front part of the plane had to stay in place until the plane could be stopped, and the propellers quit moving. Looking back through a glass astrodome in the top of the nose of the plane, I could see two balls of humanity rolling across the ground, with an ambulance in quick pursuit. As soon as possible, all of us evacuated, ran as fast as possible and dove into a nearby ditch, in case of an explosion. The ground crews took over extinguishing the flames. Quagliano and Morrison were taken to a hospital. It was miraculous that neither of them had any more injuries than a few bruises. The heavy clothing they wore apparently provided a cushion when they bailed out!

Quagliano suffered some hurt feelings and wanted Morrison to be court martialed, saying, "Well, he could have killed me when I got kicked out." That was a true statement, but had the plane exploded before anyone could escape, we all would have been dead, so it was a moot point. No action was taken, and when our 490th Bomb Group held a reunion about 45 years later, I was astounded in talking to Mike that he had no recollection of the incident.

The plane was checked to find out what caused the fire. Results showed that aileron control cables in the right wing were installed over the top of the new gas tank. As we maneuvered around the sky, the cables cut through the rubber tank as if they were a saw, leaking gas into the wing, which ignited when the exhaust backfire occurred. Had the cables been properly placed under the tank, nothing would have happened. Two experiences of fire in flight within two months was a very sobering thought. We were lucky to get out alive.

November 25, 1944
Merseburg

This time, the "Jerries" had developed some type of smoke screen which enveloped the entire area, so our bomb drops were extremely erratic. On this mission, the anti-aircraft flak was the heaviest ever seen, and our time on the bomb run and over the target was about 15 minutes, which seemed like a lifetime. Leaving the target area, we encountered German fighters until our "little friends" engaged them in dog fights to keep them off the bombers. Hann called for a damage check from the crew, getting as far as the top turret gunner, who did not respond. I was called upon to check this situation, and found Christmas sitting up there with a stupid grin, totally oblivious to anything going on around him. A piece of shrapnel from the anti-aircraft batteries had cut his oxygen hose. At 28,000 feet, when you lose your oxygen intake, death can come quickly. He was out like a light and dying when I reached him. I grabbed an air cannister from another part of the plane just in time to bring him back to reality and save his life. Damage to the group was exceedingly heavy, with only about half of our bombers getting back. We were blessed to be one of the survivors – Merseburg was a very terrible place to go on a mission. As stated on a previous report on this target, being shot down is part of the price to be paid for being there! This raid proved that point.

December 1, 1944
Mission scrubbed

There was a mission scheduled for this date, but the 490th Bomb Group had sustained such severe loss of planes over Merseburg on November 25th, in addition to heavy damage to those lucky enough to get back to the base, it was not possible to put enough planes in the air. The weather was terrible, so between these circumstances, the mission was "scrubbed", and no one flew. Hann's comments in his diary are – *"The scrubbed missions are taking their toll on my crew. It's as hard to go through all the preparation and having it scrubbed as it is to complete it. I'm a little concerned about a couple of the boys. I couldn't blame them if they were a little Flak Happy.*

December 4, 1944
Friedburg, Germany

"We went up today, but had to go through about 15,000 feet of heavy clouds to assemble together. We would fly a given direction for about 5 minutes, do a 180 degree turn all the time climbing at a certain speed. If everybody follows perfectly we shouldn't collide with another plane forming. When we suddenly feel propeller wash from another plane, it's scary! When we broke out of the clouds and were forming with our squadron, I could

"LITTLE BROTHERS"
GUARDIAN ANGELS TO THE
BOMBERS

A B-17 with Four Beautiful P-51's Flying "Shot Gun"

This beauty is our P-47 fighter, and what a magnificent plane it was. Note how close above our wing tip it was hovering.

swear that the plane was flipping over on its back. I had heard of "vertigo", but I wasn't sure if I was experiencing it or not. I gave the plane to Pat [McEwen] and just relaxed. The feeling went away, but I checked with the doctor when we got back. He explained that it probably was caused by the stress, and it shouldn't bother me. Not very much flak, and no planes lost." Since Hann had previously expressed concern about some of the crew being afflicted and "flak happy", the obvious result of intense stress, we could all sympathize with him.

December 5, 1944
Berlin

This was a very long haul into a heavily fortified anti-aircraft area, for a target smack in the middle of this metropolis. The Germans were using their subway system to move troops from the eastern frontier where the Russian armies were rapidly moving toward the German border, transferring them en masse to the western area, where the Allied forces were slowly but surely gaining more German territory en route to meet the Russians for trying to end the war. In view of these circumstances, Berlin was a prime military target. Having reached the IP for the bomb run to Berlin, we were at the center of devastating anti-aircraft fire when heavy flak hit our plane, crippling the number 3 engine, causing the plane to veer sharply to the left. McEwen was piloting at the time and signaled Hann to take over. The plane was out of control and had lost about 1,500 feet before Hann

could get it leveled out. One of the crew called on the intercom to report that bombs on the right side of the bomb bay had not dropped as expected, so we had an engine out of commission and some bombs hung up in the fuselage, both of which were on the right side. It was no wonder that the plane had veered suddenly! After some interesting and effective work over the open bomb bay, standing on a beam in the center, 25,000 feet above the ground, some of the crew (Quagliano or Morrison) were able to release the bombs and close the bay doors with the aid of a heavy pry bar. While this was going on, we had gotten far away from the bomb train and had no idea where our group was, so we tacked on to another group for protection from fighters, but couldn't keep up. The propeller on #3 engine wouldn't feather and was shaking the plane so hard it felt like the whole ship was coming apart. Hann dove about 2,000 feet and pulled up hard to try and snap the shaft – it worked – fortunately for us, the prop soared above the plane and the shaking stopped. I have often thought this was a miraculous event, because it could easily have sheered off and cut the nose of the fuselage off, killing several or all of us instantly.

At this point, we were lower than the other bombers, did not have the power to climb back to that altitude, and could not catch up with that group. Two options were open. I recommended going to Sweden, which was the closest neutral territory. The second option was to go it alone, trying to get back to our base in England, which was a long, long haul

through terrible weather and potential problems with German fighter planes on the prowl for targets just like us! Hann felt that there was a very heavy cloud deck to fly into, which offered some cover from visibility, and decided to try for returning to the base in England. The cloud cover held up enough for us to get back to France all right, which at that time had been liberated, but by then, the number 2 engine was acting up, which was not a very comforting situation. Mike Quagliano got a radio message through to the air-sea rescue group to appraise them of our situation. We were able to let down gradually and made it across the channel, where the ground crews were waiting for us as we glided to the runway! We were thankful to get back, and lucky to be alive. This was one of the roughest missions we had flown, and everyone's nerves were completely shot. In the jargon of those days, we were accutely "flak happy".

The Red Cross girls met us with drinks of bourbon and scotch to calm us down prior to the de-briefing routine. This was a report of our knowledge of conditions relating to bombing the target, loss of bombers, strength of the German fighters, etc. Our 13th mission was over, and we were very fortunate to have survived!

December 11, 1944
Giessen, Germany

This attack was in the area of Frankfurt, about midway between the northern and southern borders of Germany, not too far

from the area of Luxemberg, so it was a fairly long distance from our base in England. Our assigned target was again to cripple railroad marshalling yards. There was heavy cloud cover to contend with, but we were able to hit our objective. No flak was encountered, so it wasn't a bad mission, by comparison with some of our other sorties.

December 12, 1944
Darmstadt, Germany

Located in the southern part of Germany, between Frankfurt and Mannheim, it was getting close to the Swiss border. Our crew led the group, but instead of bombs, we carried slivers of aluminum foil, which (when dropped) interfered with their radar systems. This ploy was to make their anti-aircraft have difficulty in pinpointing our altitude, or so we were told. Never the less, as soon as we got over the target area, we had a hit that knocked out #3 engine, which had to be feathered, and also severely damaged the electrical system controlling our navigational instrumentation. With only three engines, we could not maintain speed, had to duck out of the bomb train, and into the cloud cover to avoid enemy fighter planes in the area. Our route back to home base was impaired, with basically a radio signal to "home in on". This was located in the most southern part of England, very close to the English Channel, which was where we were headed. As navigator, it was my responsibility to get us there, so we followed the heading for some time, when I advised Hann to start letting down through the clouds. He questioned our getting that far in a relatively short time, but I advised him we had picked up a tail wing, which had helped. As we reached an altitude of 2,500 feet, we began to get hits, and it looked like fire crackers all around us. To my dismay and utter astonishment, the Nazi's had put up a radio signal in Holland on the same frequency as the one in England – we were over the Zuider Zee in enemy territory! Hann hit the deck, flying as low as possible, knowing from his infantry background that adjusting the anti-aircraft guns to our low level would take a few minutes. We climbed into some nearby clouds, but their 50 caliber machine gun shells sounded like hard rain drops on a tin roof when they hit. The number 2 engine began to sound rough, raising the question of our ability to get back to England. Hann had Quagliano try to get permission for us to land in Belgium, which was denied, so then Mike got out his rosary beads for some extra help in our hour of need.

To keep the plane airborne under these circumstances, everything on board which could be moved was jettisoned into the North Sea to lighten our load. Hann nursed the plane back to the closest possible air field, which was an English base at the mouth of Thames River, where the number 2 engine conked out going in on our approach to the runway. Fortunately, those two engines, #1 and #4, had gotten us back where we belonged!

The base at which we landed was in the Margate, Westgate area, a resort section of the coast, where in normal times there would have been a lot of activities taking place. As with any resort, there were a lot of "pubs" around, nice cottages, and a genuine group of people. However, with all the men and boys serving in military activities, things seemed rather quiet at the time we were there. We went into Margate the evening when we landed, had a few drinks to calm our nerves, and someone steered us to some place where there was a dance hall – lots of girls, but no men. I remember dancing with several of them, but for some reason, I had no shoes, so my fleece lined boots served as dancing slippers.

Upon return to the base, we found that a plane from the 490th Group had been sent down to pick us up. However, it somehow had an accident after landing, running into a truck and damaging the wing tip while going down a taxi strip. The crew on that plane must have thought the area would be a wonderful place to visit for a few days! The next day, another bomber was dispatched to take our crew and the other group back to the 490th base. It was a wild and wooly experience, and again, we were lucky!

December 24, 1944
Rhein Main

This location is in the Frankfurt area, where we had been previously on the 11th and 12th of December. The mission may be best described by Hann's comments in his diary. *"We had four squadrons instead of the normal three. I think we were the only bomb group to hit the airfield. Something big is about to happen."* Short and to the point.

Other than the normal lousy weather, it was a relatively uneventful trip.

Long after the fact, Milo Simecek expressed his recollection of this experience in 1999 when we broke out of the clouds over Holland December 12, 1944. Quoting him, from his vantage point in the tail gun position, we were flying so low the farmers in their fields tending their cows were waving to us. He could also see the German soldiers in their flak towers watching us fly, but we were too low for them to shoot at us. Being so close to the surface of the North Sea, spray was clouding up our windows in the fuselage, so he climbed out of the tail gun position. When he and Quagliano met, Mike was pretty excited as we all were. Ahead of us, they could see the Cliffs of Dover, which provided a beacon for us to head for.

Planes on way to the target leaving trails. Note what appears to be 12 B-17 bombers heading "home" in opposite direction at lower level.

Con-trails clearly point out location of bombers for anti-aircraft artillery as they head for targets. Note two planes at lower level returning from target leave no trails.

CHAPTER 7
THE CHRISTMAS CRASH

On December 25, 1944, the 8th Air Force was scheduled to bomb a target at Ahrweiler, Germany. Our crew was assigned to be a part of this attack, which involved every plane available to fly.

Our ground troops had crossed France and Belgium, with heavy inroads into German territory. This unexpected invasion of their territory required troops from all over Germany, Poland, and other areas to be rushed into action to stop the Allied Forces on their trek to conquer Berlin. This became known as "The Battle of the Bulge," where the Germans had successfully surrounded our troops, cutting off all supplies of food, ammunition, medical supplies, etc. Help was desperately needed, and aerial combat support was the only apparent alternative.

The weather all over Europe was terrible. Ice and snow was everywhere. Temperatures were at sub-freezing levels over the entire continent, with fog and low clouds so thick you could hardly see your hand in front of your face. Vehicles and personnel were stopped "dead in their tracks". Conditions with our troops in the "Bulge" were so desperate that 8th Air Force had to order the mission, in spite of the weather.

Our crew, as well as many others, was awakened very early to prepare for the flight. Breakfast was somber that day, followed by the briefing session to learn where and what we would be bombing as the target. The usual procedure identified the encircled location, with data on German troop locations around the perimeter. We also learned that the Germans had already demanded a surrender of our forces, but the General in command of our troops responded with a single word – "Nuts". It was not a pretty picture.

The weather officers gave us the report on flying conditions, which we already knew from being out in the ice, snow, sleet, fog, and low level clouds. As a practical matter, everyone received the encouraging news that there was no known place to land anywhere on the continent. This meant England was the only alternative, but the senior officer in charge advised that flight crews returning from the mission would be very fortunate to find such a location! At this point orders were received from a very high level commands that as a last resort, put the plane on automatic pilot, head it out over the North Sea, and bail out by parachute over England! Such an order was unthinkable, but bore out the urgency of what we were trying to accomplish.

When the briefing was over, I went back to the barracks and picked up a bottle of Johnny Walker Red Label Scotch – just it case it was needed. After that, I went to the flight line and the hard stand where our bomber was parked. In a short time, orders from the control tower instructed us to move out to a specific taxi strip, in preparation for take-off. Hann's comments were, *"It was so foggy I couldn't see the wing tips."* In the nose position, I was looking out the Plexiglas to try and see a red light on the tail of a plane just 50 feet ahead of us, but couldn't see it. The ground and all of the concrete strips were slippery with ice and frost, so even though the planes had just been de-iced for take-off, all of the surfaces were impaired again. Hann sent Christmas out on the runway to try and get the plane straight on the runway so that he could take off using the direction indicator, and a lot of prayers. Hann's further description covers the course of events. *"When I hit about 75 miles per hour, I knew we were off the runway. I couldn't lift off at that speed, so I throttled back and yelled to Pat to pull the wheels out from under us. Christmas fired a red flare, and about that time it felt like we had gone over a stump or something. Number 2 engine was smoking, and we came to a sudden stop."* The sudden bump referred to may have been when the bottom gun turret got ripped out.

On board we had 12 bombs suspended in racks inside the bomb bay. Each of these weighed 500 pounds and obviously had been jarred quite a bit, so they were very dangerous. In addition, the gas tanks in the wings contained 2,800 gallons of 100 octane gas. Everyone knew that an explosion could occur at any moment, so evacuation was paramount. The guys in the rear of the plane could get out through the rear door. For the two pilots, navigator, and bombardier in the forward section of the plane, it was more complicated. Up in the nose, it seemed that the fuselage was on the ground, so the escape hatch in the bottom of the plane was impractical. The other option was the celestial astro-dome (a glass bubble in the roof of the plane) which included a hinged door for opening. The bombardier got there first, but with all the heavy clothing, he got stuck in the opening. I was impatient, wanted out, and kicked the guy in the seat of his pants so hard he went out like greased lightning, and I was right behind him. He jumped off the right side, so I went left to avoid landing on top of him. Unfortunately, there was a drainage ditch on that side, covered with ice and snow. Upon impact, I went into the water, and by the time I could get out, my clothes were so water logged I couldn't stand up. Some of the crew rushed to help me, thinking I was badly injured. Hann, in trying to get out of the pilot's seat, found the same ditch. When someone helped him out of the water, we all ran and hid behind a large mound of dirt, wondering when the plane would blow up. After what seemed an eternity, several jeeps picked us up. After being checked for injuries, we were told that as soon as our crash occurred, the entire 8th Air Force was scrubbed and the planes were grounded. At that point, I went back for my bottle of Scotch and we all drank it.

This was a terrible experience! A majority of people in plane crashes do not survive. Some few may. In retrospect, I had to wonder about the odds of surviving the fiery ride back from Kassel on October 2, the freak fire on the test flight of November 22, and now this crash on take-off December 25, 1944?

For Hann's crew, it was a wonderful present few people would ever have. It was a merry Christmas.

CHRISTMAS DAY 1944,
CRASH ON TAKE-OFF EFFORT
TO HELP TROOPS IN
"BATTLE OF THE BULGE"

This close up vividly shows snow, ice and mud, as well as #3 engine dragging the ground. Art Dersham's picture.

Plane came to rest in ditch on left side – 6,000 pounds of bombs and 2,800 gallons of gas somehow did not explode. Miraculous!

Note #3 Engine ripped from wing engine mount on right side. It took a lot of pressure to do that! The plane was only gook for spare parts!

#2 Engine on left side lost cowling cover & bent props before coming to rest in the ditch. Note upper gun turret on top of fuselage.

Standing in front of Christmas Day Crash. Left to right (Standing): Simecek, Quagliano, McEwen. Front: Christmas, Morrison. All of crew were very lucky survivors 1944.

CHAPTER 8

HAPPY NEW YEAR

1945 ROLLED AROUND

With the advent of this New Year, the stress and strain from experiences of the past months had begun to show. We were all pretty "Flak Happy", showing fatigue, with nerves strung to the breaking point, and most everyone having the shakes frequently. One of the crew reached a point where getting into the plane made him violently ill. We definitely needed to "get away from it all".

Hann, McEwen, Cooper, and I were sent to a "flak shack" at Lands End, England. This rest home was in reality a beautiful mansion on a large estate in a rural setting of the English countryside. It was reportedly owned by someone who was part of the British royalty. The other crewmembers were sent to another rest home for their recuperation.

Upon our arrival at our new quarters, each of us was issued very casual civilian clothing, something we had not seen in quite a while. Getting out of uniform seemed a great way to start our relaxation. The other amenities included athletics such as tennis, golf, and long walks through beautiful gardens. For those interested in reading, there was a huge library, and anyone who liked horseback riding simply went to the stable. The food was excellent – breakfast, lunch, and dinner were all served on linen tablecloths with fine silverware. Not many excellent hotels could have matched the décor we enjoyed.

As we approached the weekend, rumors began to circulate that on Saturday night, there would be a big dance, with girls from the local area and those serving in nearby military functions having been invited to the party. This prompted a small group to make a quick trip into London to pick up some libation for the gathering. Little did they know just how much booze the U.S. Government had available, but it was plenty. Everyone had all the drinks they could handle, the party was enjoyed by all, and we, as those sent for rehabilitation, had made great progress in recovering from our "flak happy" status. At the end of the week, we returned to the 490th Group for active duty. Upon arrival, we found a new crew sharing the Quonset hut with us. Hodges, who had been with us, and his crew had been shot down, along with four other crews in our group. He had been flying in the position normally assigned to Hann. This was a rough awakening for our return, but we had dodged another life threatening situation. The Flak Shack saved us.

Our war resumed on January 14, 1945, when we were assigned to a raid on oil storage areas at Derban, Germany. Located about 25 mile west of Berlin, this target was heavily fortified with anti-aircraft, and another very long mission. Over the target, we were again hit, with #3 engine taken out and feathered. This seemed to be a replay of our mission to Berlin on December 5, 1944. Looking back over our missions, it's interesting to note that the #3 engine got hit quite a few times. Returning on three engines for such a long distance, with the usual weather problems, German fighters attacking the bomb train, and dealing with other little surprises which always seem to occur, was no fun. We did make it back, however, and were glad to have one more mission behind us.

January 15, 1945
Augsburg, Germany

This was a long haul, very near to Munich, Germany, and about 2,000 miles for the round trip. There was heavy cloud cover, so confirming destruction of the target was difficult. We saw black smoke coming up through the clouds, and Hann's comment was, "We probably knocked the hell out of the whole city", which may very easily have happened. We did not experience any flak holes in the plane. This mission, on the heels of our raid on Derben yesterday, meant that we had covered about 3,800 miles in these missions, back to back. That's a VERY rough schedule. Our P-51 fighters were reported to have shot down 183 German fighter planes – Hann said he saw one of them go down, so everyone had a bad day.

January 16, 1945
Bitterfeld, Germany

This target was east of Leipzig, the site of a large chemical plant, which we plastered. The mission itself was rather routine, but to think that we flew the 14th, 15th, and 16th – three combat missions in a row, for a total aggregate of about 5,500 miles, mostly over enemy territory, is unbelievable!! To put this in perspective, we probably were awakened about 4:00 a.m., went through the routine, including briefing, and got off the runway around 6:30 a.m. The assembly, make up of the bomb train, flight to and from the target, probably took about 9 hours. Upon return, we went to debriefing to report our analysis of the mission, which required a while, then to our barracks to clean up a little before going to the officers club, where all of the combat group gathered to have a few drinks to relax, swap stories of what we each saw, or had happen to us, etc. From there everyone went to the mess hall, since about 5:00 a.m. no one had anything to eat, and by the time supper was finished, it was quite likely to be around 9:00 p.m. If your crew was on standby, the usual format was to post notices, so those involved could retire around 10:00 p.m. Theoretically, this would provide 6 hours for sleeping, but I never knew anyone who had flown a mission and was able to relax very well afterward. So, in the case of these three days, no one got much rest, a lot of drinks were consumed to deal with the strain, and upon entering the plane, everyone put on their mask and breathed in 100% oxygen for a while to feel human and prepare for the events of that day.

Only because we were all in our late teens and early twenties could we have had the stamina to fight under such conditions. To top it all off, when we returned from this particular mission, we could not land at our own base near Eye, and got diverted to a place named Ricall, about 170 miles northeast of there. What a day that was!

January 20, 1945
Rheine, Germany

We had hardly gotten to sleep when the flashlight guy came through the hut and woke us up. Our briefing was at 3:00 a.m., a VERY EARLY call for any mission. Our crew was flying deputy lead for the 490th group, which was leading the entire 8th Air Force, something we had never done before. This put us

Smoke rising from the targets provided evidence of success at Manheim – January 21, 1945 Dersham's picture.

in a very positive leadership position where there could be no errors. This was a very unusual mission, with a schedule for night take-offs and assembly – not a routine procedure. After getting all the planes airborne, the formation of the bomb stream commenced and being the lead group, we headed toward Germany, with the other groups falling in behind us. Over the Channel, unfortunately, our #4 engine caught fire. We were able to extinguish it, but upon efforts to restart, the fire was again ignited. Number 3 engine was running rough, and the propeller was running away. We had no alternative but to abort, drop the bombs in the Channel, and return to the base. The temperature was 58 degrees below zero at flight altitude of 27,000 feet. We were sorry to go through all the pre-flight, assembly, etc., then not be able to participate in what was an eventful mission – not to mention that the opportunity to lead the 8th Air Force to the target wouldn't occur again. (It didn't).

January 21, 1945 – Manheim - Luwingshaven

Since we didn't complete the flight to Rheine on the day before, someone decided we should fly this mission. Thanks a lot, whoever you were!

This target was deep into southern Germany, at a point where the boundaries of both France and Switzerland were very close. The weather was terrible. We climbed through 22,000 feet of soup, along with the other 1,200 bombers on this maximum effort mission, before breaking out into clear skies. Imagine all of those planes "climbing the lad-

B-17's flying over the Alps.

der" simultaneously to regroup and form the bomb train. With this type activity in such limited space that airfields were almost on top of each other, it's amazing what was done!

When the bomb train was assembled, we headed southeast to Germany, where our initial point for the bomb run was very close to the Swiss border. The Swiss Alps were in clear view, and made a wonderful storybook picture. However, when you looked ahead toward the target, a gruesome experience was unfolding. We were in the area of exceedingly heavy flak and the bomber in front of us, one of our own group, received a direct hit and exploded. Debris was scattered all over the sky, and how we avoided being hit with the results of this carnage is unkonwn. From the nose of our plane no parachutes were seen. Such an experience as this remains with you a long, long time! We found a few holes in our plane, but sure sweated out that bomb run. As soon as the bombs were dropped, we took evasive action out of there and pointed our nose toward England. It was a long way back through dense clouds, looking out to avoid collision with other bombers, and dwelling too much on what we had just been through! We finally made it back to the 490th air base, and were darned glad to be there!

January 22, 1945
This was the best assignment we had received for a while, considering the activities involving 5 missions in the compressed time of the past 8 days – we were relieved from duty and given a 48 hour pass to London. In spite of the war, blackouts to try and prevent excessive bombing, limited transportation facilities, restaurants advertising great steaks, which in all probability were horse meat, and other things of similar nature, it was a great metropolis for relaxation. Hotels were plentiful and always treated military personnel very graciously. Piccadilly was always jumping with people wandering from one entertainment feature to another, lots of shows, and plenty of girls hanging around waiting for some GI to strike up a conversation and offer to buy them a drink. One of the shows I remember was a beautiful girl appearing in different nude, or semi-nude, poses behind a framed-in stage, with lights being turned on in a rather subdued light, and then turned off very quickly. This format included quite a num-

ber of frames, and always seemed to have a full, attentive audience, but you had to be quick to really see the show! When the war was over and I returned home, a friend of mine was talking to me about his experiences in London, and this subject came up. This fellow was inducted into the Army the same day I was, and all of his friends were amazed, since he had lost sight in one eye during his childhood and everyone thought that would automatically keep him out of the draft. No so – the Army decided he could do clerical work quite well, so he ended up in the European Theater with a lot of others. On his way to France, he passed through London, and yes, he well remembered that particular show. His comment to me was ,"I did go to see it, but as you know, I have only one good eye, and before I could get it focused on the framed picture, they turned the damned lights off." I could sympathize with him, but always got a laugh out of our conversation. In any event, getting away from bombing missions for a short time was always a delightful escape.

January 26, 1945
Wesel, Germany

Everyone scheduled to fly had been awakened earlier, had breakfast, gone to the briefing session, and prepared for combat. By the time we reached the hardstand where our planes awaited, 8th Air Force Headquarters had scrubbed the mission. Heavy fog, freezing frost and ice conditions, along with terribly bad weather, had over-ruled the military objectives for that day.

January 28, 1945
Scrubbed Mission

The snow was coming down so heavily, visibility was absolute zero. That English weather was something else!

January 29, 1945
Koblenz, Germany

This mission went into the area southeast of the site where the "Battle of the Bulge" took place at Christmas time. After the routine wake-up, breakfast, briefing, take-off, and climbing the ladder for assembly in the bomb train, trouble reared its ugly head. The supercharger on #3 engine failed to function, making it impossible to keep up with the group. Hann decided to tack on to another group, but this didn't work out any better, and it was necessary to jettison six 500 pound bombs to lighten the load enough to keep up with that group. Two bombers collided at the assembly point, just a bright orange flash. No chutes were seen, again displaying the dangers preparing for flights to the target. Christmas and I did not fly this mission due to illness.

February 3, 1945
Big Berlin

After our previous missions to this place, we knew it would be a very rough mission, with a maximum effort of at least 1,000 planes to make our presence known. A subsequent report in the Stars and Stripes newspaper, which appeared two days later, confirmed that more than 1,000 bombers were involved.

Also mentioned was the fact that this bomb train stretched almost 300 miles across the continent and required 45 minutes to rain 2,500 tons of bombs on the target. A copy of this news report is attached as a matter of interest. At this period in the war, German troops were still being transferred from Poland and Russia to the western front, where they were losing ground to Allied forces.

Our briefing for this mission assigned us to hit the Teargarden Subway entrance, in the middle of Berlin, almost adjacent to Hitler's headquarters. This place was packed with people trying to get out of the path of the Russians moving against this capitol, as well as German troops being transported through there. This was the first time any of us had given any thought to civilians being caught in activities of war, but the Germans had not been concerned about that in bombing our targets, so it was just an unfortunate aspect of war. One of our planes from the 490th Bomb Group was hit over the target and decided to head for Russian in an effort to survive. All of us thought about this crew, wondering if they could make it to some safe landing area, and keeping our fingers crossed for their survival. (On March 30, 1945, we got word that they did survive and were able to get back to England. A remarkable achievement!)

This mission to Berlin was another long haul for our crew, about 1,800 miles total, with the usual flak, stress, and strain of combat conditions, and a very trying experience. We were glad to just get back to our base and friendly territory.

New York   London Edition   Paris

THE STARS AND STRIPES

Extra   Daily Newspaper of U.S. Armed Forces   in the European Theater of Operations   Extra

VOL. 5 No. 86—14.   MONDAY, Feb. 5, 1945

anila Entered: 1st Breaks Siegfried Be

This remarkable picture of the assault on Berlin shows the con-trails, due to atmospheric conditions.This pinpointed the exact position of each plane, benefiting anti-aircraft ground crews. Hann's crew was on this mission, having a target in Downtown Berlin – the Teargarden Subway system, being used for the movement of German troops. As described further in the report, this was a very difficult mission.

February 6, 1945

We had a 48 hour pass and took off for London to enjoy a different lifestyle from flying bombers! The target for this date, if we had been scheduled to fly, was Chemnitz, Germany. The ladder climb to reach the assembly was reported to have been hectic, and somewhere going into the bomb train, one of the pilots from our squadron collided with another plane. All members of that crew, except the ball turret gunner, were able to bail out. It wasn't a good situation to lose one of the crew, or the plane, but we were blessed to have been "off duty" that day.

February 14, 1945
Valentine's Day

Our present was the "opportunity" to go back to Chemnitz, since we missed the mission of February 6. This target was located just about to the border of Czechoslovakia, south of Dresden, which probably was 900 to 1,000 miles each way. As usual, the weather was terrible getting airborne from home base, and the route to the target was just about as bad. We flew about 600 miles through a front, flying in formation, which was very risky, and encountered persistent con-trails, a weather condition leaving vapor trails behind the planes, which made them easy targets for anti-aircraft flak. Hann's diary shows that our flight time in these conditions was about 8 hours, and because of the weather conditions, our wing man lost us, which contributed to the mission being a real mess. We managed to get over the target, drop our bomb load, and get out of there, but not without picking up some holes in the plane. Coming away from the bomb run, we were hit hard in areas not expected to give us any problems, which scared the hell out of us. One of our group, piloted by a fellow named Muir, caught some flak which knocked an engine out and wounded the nose gunner on his crew. He did manage to straggle back across the German border and land in Brussels. We were able to get back to our base in England. As Hann stated, *"This might be a day for romance for some, but this is about the roughest mission I've had."*

February 16, 1945
Hamm, Germany

THE
PRESIDENT
OF
THE UNITED STATES OF AMERICA

To all who shall see these presents, greeting:

Know Ye, that reposing special trust and confidence in the patriotism, valor, fidelity and abilities of EMANUEL JOSEPH JOHNSON, JUNIOR

I do appoint him FIRST LIEUTENANT, AIR CORPS *in the*

Army of the United States

such appointment to date from the TWENTIETH *day of* SEPTEMBER *nineteen hundred and* FORTY-FIVE *He is therefore carefully and diligently to discharge the duty of the office to which he is appointed, by doing and performing all manner of things thereunto belonging.*

He will enter upon active duty under this commission only when specifically ordered to such active duty by competent authority.

And I do strictly charge and require all Officers and Soldiers under his command when he shall be employed on active duty, to be obedient to his orders as an officer of his grade and position. And he is to observe and follow such orders and directions from time to time, as he shall receive from me, or the future President of the United States of America, or the General or other Superior Officers set over him, according to the rules and discipline of War.

This Commission evidences an appointment in the Army of the United States, under the provisions of section 37, National Defense Act, as amended, and is to continue in force for a period of five years from the date above specified, and during the pleasure of the President of the United States, for the time being.

Done at the City of Washington, this THIRTEENTH *day of* DECEMBER *in the year of our Lord one thousand nine hundred and* FORTY-FIVE *, and of the Independence of the United States of America the one hundred and* SEVENTIETH *.*

By the President:

Adjutant General.

118

This was located in the Ruhr Valley, not too far from our first target, October 2, 1944 when we hit Kassel. This section of Germany was fairly close to the border of Belgium, so the distance was not excessive. The weather had cleared, for a change, and we could actually see the target – railroad marshalling yards, which we clobbered. Considering that we had taken off in fog and flown through overcast most of the way, having clear skies for our bomb drop was a pleasant surprise! Our encounter with flak was moderate, and we didn't loiter in that area, heading for England. The return trip was the same weather we had left earlier, and conditions for landing were a 300 foot ceiling, with 1,500-foot visibility! All of our planes landed safely in

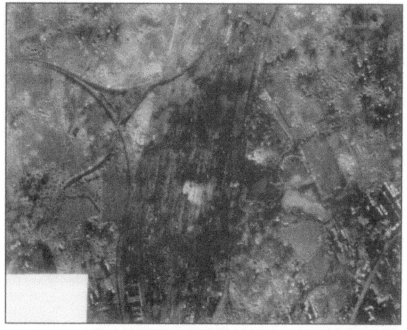

Railroad marshalling yard at Hamm, Germany. Taken from 25,000 feet by Art Dersham.

spite of the lousy weather.

CHAPTER 9

AN EIGHTH AIR FORCE BOMBER STATION, ENGLAND--OVER 70 TONS OF HIGH EXPLOSIVES HAVE BEEN DROPPED ON GERMAN MILITARY AND INDUSTRIAL INSTALLATIONS BY THE CREW OF THE EIGHTH AIR FORCE B-17 FLYING FORTRESS "FLAK HAPPY," OF WHICH FIRST LIEUTENANT EMANUEL J. JOHNSON, JR., 21, OF FERNANDINA, FLA., IS NAVIGATOR.

FLYING OVER 20,000 MILES IN MORE THAN 30 HIGH ALTITUDE COMBAT MISSIONS WITH THE 490TH BOMB. GROUP, LT. JOHNSON HAS BEEN DECORATED SIX TIMES -- HE HOLDS THE AIR MEDAL WITH FIVE OAK LEAF CLUSTERS FOR "MERITORIOUS ACHIEVEMENT."

HE HAS TAKEN PART IN BOMBING ATTACKS ON OIL REFINERIES AT MERSEBURG AND LUDWIGSHAVEN, ORDNANCE DEPOTS AT BERLIN AND TANK FACTORIES AT KASSEL.

"THE TIME WE BOMBED TANK FACTORIES AT KASSEL STANDS OUT IN MY MIND AS BEING THE ROUGHEST MISSION," SAID LT. JOHNSON. "WE TRAVELED
LEFT
OVER 600 MILES WITH OUT KNOWING THAT OUR/WING WAS BURNING INTERNALLY AFTER BEING HIT BY FLAK."

LT. JOHNSON IS THE SON OF MR. AND MRS. EMANUEL J. JOHNSON, SR. OF 6085 FLETCHER AVENUE, FERNANDINA, AND PRIOR TO ENTERING THE ARMY AIR FORCES IN FEBRUARY, 1943, HE WAS EMPLOYED BY THE RAYONIER COMPANY INC.

THE 490TH BOMB. GROUP IS A UNIT OF THE THIRD AIR DIVISION, THE DIVISION CITED BY THE PRESIDENT FOR ITS HISTORIC ENGLAND-AFRICA SHUTTLE BOMBING OF MESSERSCHMITT AIRCRAFT PLANTS AT REGENSBURG GER....

This copy of an 8th Air Force news release verifies that an average mission exceeded 600 miles... most of which, was over enemy territory. Missions usually took 8 to 12 hours to complete.

CHANGING TIMES

RECONNAISANCE MISSIONS, "V.E. DAY", AND THE GERMAN SURRENDER

After our mission to Hamm on February 16, prior discussions continued between

Hann and Major Cochran regarding the possibility of our crew transferring from the 490th combat activities to a weather reconnaissance operation for the 8th Air Force. One of the considerations involved which crewmembers would be transferred. On February 17, these problems were solved, with most of the crew intact, except the bombardier, who was not required for this new type operation. On February 19, 1945, we took off from our air base at Diss in a beat up, war weary B-17 and headed for the Headquarters, 3rd Scouting Force, 862nd Bombardment Squadron at a field in southern England, near the Thames River, which turned out to be primarily a P-51 fighter group base – our "Little Friends", where we checked in for duty.

No one knew exactly what this transfer entailed, but we did know that our future flights would be in brand new, stripped down B-17s, with no armament, not even a pistol, for protection. This modification increased the speed of the plane to about 200 miles per hour, quite a step upward from what we had been flying. We all felt that whatever the program, it had to be better than the combat conditions we had been involved with to complete all of our previous missions.

Our indoctrination cleared up a lot of uncertainties and was very enlightening. We would be flying night time missions to check out the weather conditions en route to targets previously selected by 8th Air Force Headquarters and reporting back to a command center on what we found. Decisions would then be made to order groups to fly that day, or scrub the mission due to inclement weather conditions. These weather reconnaissance activities were coordinated with the P-51 group in many instances. If the proposed bomb target was deep into enemy territory, the P-51's, which were lighter and faster than our B-17 would go much deeper into Germany, relaying information back to our plane, which then advised the command center, so it became a coordinated relay system.

Obviously, with the unpredictable weather conditions in England, our flights in this new environment dictated take-offs and landings in any and all extremes. This could be very tricky, and sometimes required finding alternate bases clear enough to permit landing. So, it wasn't exactly a "Bed of Roses". In addition to these activities, we were called upon to provide taxi services for Generals who needed to go somewhere, like Paris and other interesting locations, or for aerial inspection trips, all of which were interesting.

These flights were unlike bombing sorties, in that there was only one B-17 flying to check out the weather, rather than assembling 1,000 bombers for combat, so this time aloft was much shorter. We might leave on a mission at 4:00 a.m. and return to the base by 7:30 a.m., for instance, having completed our objective and reported on the weather.

The lifestyle at this base seemed to be more casual, without the pressure experienced under combat conditions. The fighter pilots were all great guys – they loved flying those P-51's and they thoroughly enjoyed parties. There were several bases nearby where a lot of girls were involved with hospital operations and other duties where the English people had put many women into service dealing with routine activities, such as keeping records, driving cars and ambulances, handling clerical duties, etc. So it was never a problem to get up an impromptu party.

While most of our reconnaissance flights were pretty routine, some had exceedingly interesting aspects which bear reporting.

One of these flights was to Denmark, where the Germans had extensive submarine facilities bordering on the North Sea. This was an excellent site for quick submersion of their subs, and had direct access to the North Atlantic under water, thus avoiding the likelihood of aerial observation as to their whereabouts. These sub pens were huge, constructed out of reinforced concrete of such density that any bombs dropped from planes would have practically no affect on them. While our air forces and ground troops were making good progress in efforts to defeat the Germans, their subs were taking a heavy toll on our shipping efforts. No one really knows what these losses were, but all materials being transported across the Atlantic were vital to ending the war, so it was imperative to try and eliminate as many of their submarines as possible.

Knowing that the sub pens were impenetrable under normal attack procedures, the thought was that perhaps low flying bombers might be able to execute some "skip bombing", whereby the bombs would be dropped from a very low level and skim across the North Sea surface into the pens for destruction of both the subs and the protective pens. Another alternative was to use torpedoes launched from low flying planes to penetrate the target, as had been proven successful in the Pacific Theater operations. Our mission on this particular day was to explore how, and if, this could be done. It was pitch black dark, and we had to fly right on top of the North Sea to avoid being spotted by their radar. Due to the darkness and zero altitude above the water, this was an exceedingly dangerous and risky mission. It was a pretty scary experience, but we did accomplish the objective of getting close enough to effectively drop the bombs, or torpedoes, had that been part of the program, and we avoided being caught by their defense aircraft. Our return trip to home base was through exceedingly bad weather, which was very turbulent and tricky, leading to a really rough landing. One of the P-51's flying at the same time crashed on landing strictly due to the weather, so we were lucky. We never heard if the information we reported about this mission led to a raid on that target, but we think our experience proved that bombing the sub pens could be done!!

Shortly after this adventure, we received an assignment to go to Paris and pick up a

DAILY EXPRESS

No. 14,018   Coast dim-out 10.20 pm to 5.32 am   **WEDNESDAY MAY 9 1945**   Moon rises 6.5 am (Thurs) sets 7.43 pm   One Penny

The picture that tells it all: Churchill in the midst of the people

THIS WAS THEIR
FINEST DAY

**And Monty gives
final message**

Well done:
Good luck
to you all

FIELD-MARSHAL SIR BERNARD
MONTGOMERY and General Eisen-
hower last night gave their personal
thanks as man to man to the troops
who fought under them and won the
war in Europe.

Monty said : Let us embark on what lies
ahead full of joy and optimism. We have won,
the German war, let us now win the peace.
Good luck to you all, wherever you may be.

The Supreme Commander
wrote : The crusade on which
we embarked in the early
summer of 1944 has reached
its glorious conclusion. Every
man, every woman, of every
nation represented in this
command has served according to his or her ability

Here is what Montgomery
said on this day of victory to

3 a.m. LATEST

New York   London Edition   Paris

VE-DAY   # THE STARS AND STRIPES   **VE-DAY**

Daily Newspaper of U.S. Armed Forces   in the European Theater of Operations
VAT'S No. 158—1d.   **TUESDAY, MAY 8, 1945** ★

GERMANY
QUITS

Today, May 8, is VE-Day, and will be officially proclaimed so by the leaders of the Big Three in
simultaneous declarations in Washington, London and Moscow.

This was announced last night, following unofficial celebrations yesterday afternoon throughout the world, inspired by a

General, who needed a ride back to England. It was an interesting trip. Upon arrival at the French Air Base, we were surprised to see quite a few German airplanes, some of which were new, all parked side by side. While we never had an official explanation of why they were there, we concluded that these planes were probably flown by German pilots who wanted to defect and become prisoners of war, since things were going very badly for the Germans at that time. We found that the General who was to be our passenger had arranged for us to have some free time, so we went into Paris. After doing some browsing through stores, even though none of us knew any French, we hailed a taxi and somehow got the message across that we wanted to find a nice restaurant. Imagine our surprise when he delivered us to "Maxim's," which was probably the finest restaurant in France at that time! The only thing any of us could recognize on the menu was the word "lobster", so we had that for lunch! From there, we took the subway to Versailles, the site of a palace built by Louis XIV, where the peace treaty was signed by the Allies and Germany in 1919 to end World War I. It was a beautiful place, and very interesting to see. The subway got us back in time to meet the General at the appointed hour, and we headed back to London. We expressed our appreciation to the General for a delightful day!

On another occasion, we had some time off from regular duties, so we headed for Ireland in a B-17 borrowed from Uncle Sam, which was not in use at that time. In those days, during the 1944-1945 era, the southern part of Ireland was considered to be sympathetic to the German/Axis movement, so any visitation by our military personnel to that section was totally "off limits". In fact, my recollection is that any contact there would be construed as being sympathetic to the enemy, leading to a court-martial offense. Consequently, we headed to Belfast in Northern Ireland, where the people welcomed us with open arms. (In this era of the 1990's, the Southern part of Ireland is recommended for tourists, due to the civil unrest between Catholics and other factions within the Northern Ireland region. How times change!!)

For this trip, Hann, Johnson, and Major Ryan all stuck together as sightseers and travelers. We had meals of real eggs, steaks, and fresh fish, along with other delightful dishes not available in our GI meals back at the base. The Grand Central there was a nice hotel in the downtown area where we stayed. We paraded around the town in a horse and buggy, took a lot of pictures, and went out into the countryside to see the houses with thatched roofs, and saw folks using peat, which we had never seen before, as a source for lighting fires, etc.

Hann reports in his diary that on our return to the hotel, we had a nice dinner in the dining room and later wound up having a party in our room. I don't know who joined us for the social activities, but evidently some folks did, though no clues were provided on that point. He did state that when he woke up the next morning, the Major was sleeping on the mattress on the floor, and I was reclined on top of bare springs. It sounds like quite a party –sorry I don't remember any of it. The next day, we brought two Army nurses and a WAC back to England with us. Hann took them to dinner at the post and saw them off to London. Several pictures are included herein to show part of the Ireland visit.

In April of 1945, a lot of things kept coming forth to show indications of the Germans being under intensive pressure. The Allied forces were capturing larger segments of ground territory, and the superior might of our Air Force continued to shoot down German fighter plans in numbers of 75 to 100, or more, on a daily basis. Reports continued to be heard of heavy advances by the Russians on the eastern front in the region of Poland, and fuel for German operations was too scarce to permit them to do normal activities. All these conditions meant that our forces needed observation of areas no longer involved with heavy fighting, so our scouting force became more active with daylight flights. On April 17, we flew to Cologne and the entire surrounding area at very low levels to tour as a sight seeing and photo mission. Considering the times we had bombed that target and experienced the heavy flak concentrations, it seemed unreal to be just cruising around as we were. While it was evident that certain sections of Cologne had sustained heavy bombing damage, it was remarkable to see that nothing had happened to damage the beautiful cathedral there with its tall spires.

During the period covering the last couple of weeks in April and the first week of May, we made a few more trips to Paris providing taxi service for the command officers, and it became more obvious that the war was winding down. On April 29, 1945, we heard an announcement at 4:00 a.m. of an Armistice being signed, but this was later found to be a false report.

Our last, and perhaps most interesting, reconnaissance flight was on May 8, 1945. This was "V.E. Day" with the cessation of all combat activities terminating at 8:00 a.m. that morning. We were flying over Holland in the early pre-dawn hours monitoring weather conditions there and reporting back to Air Force Headquarters. At that point in time, the people of Holland had become impoverished, and in a great many circumstances were approaching starvation levels, resulting from German exploitation of food supplies raised in Holland.

The English, Americans, and other Allies had determined to overcome this problem as soon as the war was over. Accordingly, based upon our reports of clear weather all over Holland, this rescue program was put into immediate action. Every plane that could fly did so, carrying loads of food and, wherever possible, towing a glider behind it. Promptly at 8:00 a.m., thousands of aircraft of every description flew in at very low levels, dropping by parachutes these supplies for the people of Holland who waited by the thousands for this vital rescue mission. At that time of the year, the beautiful flowers Holland is noted for were all in majestic bloom, and it was a sight such as no one had ever seen. To be part of this final act of mercy at the end of a war where millions of people had been sacrificed was overwhelming!!

Based upon all the circumstances, it appears that "Hann's Crew" probably had a place in history as the last American bomber over enemy occupied territory in Holland prior to the 8:00 a.m. official surrender, and the first American plane over the free European Theater at 8:01 a.m. that day of May 8, 1945.

We flew back to our base in England and went into London to help celebrate the occasion. What an experience that was!!!

HANN'S DIARY MAY 16, 1945

This will be my last entry since things have become very dull and uninteresting. I'm all packed and have cleared the field. Waiting for orders to go home. I pitched the baseball game yesterday and won my own game with a double in the 9th inning with two men on. Now that my combat is over, at least for a few months, I'm gaining weight and feeling better in general. Nobody but one of us knows what a relief it is to know that Jerry won't be around to clobber you out of the sky. Sometimes I wonder how we ever managed to get back all the time. A couple of the boys will never be able to fly combat again. Johnson, Morrison, and Simecek are all, as we term it "Flak Happy" and were flying on sheer guts. Christmas has gone bananas since I left the crew. He is a good engineer but a hard kid to handle. I doubt that he'll keep his stripes very long when he gets back to the states. As for the rest, they came over here boys, but are going back men. I'll never forget this crew as long as I live and I thank the good Lord that they all got back in one piece. I know I've changed, but to what degree I'll never know. No doubt combat has left its mark.

In this diary I have given a very brief account of some of our missions, but it doesn't really tell the story, so just for posterity (I might have children someday) I'll go through a mission from the beginning.

Sometime between 0100 hours and 0400 hours we were awakened for a briefing. The times, weather, route, target, and expected opposition was explained to us. We then dressed for altitude coldness and went out to the ship. With everything checked and in order, we taxied out to take off at a briefed time.

All of us "sweated out" a takeoff with a full load of gasoline and bombs. Many planes exploded before they had gotten two miles. Bad visibility, ice on the wings and the runways caused most of this. We assembled anywhere between 6,000' to 25,000'. Going up through overcast, often as much as 15,000' thick, planes would collide and never know what hit them. It wasn't unusual to find ourselves in propwash and never see the other plane. The assembly itself was tricky, with a heavy plane and a whole division in one area, they often collided.

Going across the Channel was a breathing spell until we got over enemy territory. We could always see our fighter cover. Unless our group was first over, the target was usually black with flak. To be able to see the stuff for fifty miles or so, and know we were going straight into it, was something only we know. One of the boys would call-out, "The bomber's going down in flame" and our dogfights trying to keep Jerry fighters from getting to us. The bomb bays open and we're in the flak, and a bunch of prayers are being said. Pieces of flak rattle when it hits the plane, but all is forgotten except having a tight formation so that the trip won't be in vain. At last, bomb's away, it won't be long now. A quick turn, an increase in speed, change in altitude and it's all over.

The men check in any casualties and battle damage on the interphone. We then check out formation and change positions if any ships have gone down. Nothing to worry about except the lead navigator making good the flak alleys or fighters on route back. Everyone relaxes when we get back to Allied territory. The formation loosens up considerably. About 1/3 of the time we had to peel off above the clouds because we couldn't fly formation on instruments. This could make it pretty rough if one or two engines were out. Then the landing, interrogation, a shot of bourbon, a bite to eat and finally after twelve to fourteen hours of that, the sack.

After the troubles we had, is it any wonder that some of the men became extremely nervous, "flak happy". But after all is done, there's a good feeling inside, knowing that we did a good job. Buddies went down alongside us, but outside of intelligence reports to officers, nothing is said. Sometimes things are better left unsaid.

These were my thoughts and impressions, but I am sure that each of you could add your own personal feelings to these times we spent together. I hope this brings back some memories and helps to give generations to follow the feelings we had in our attempt to end the war of all wars!

CHAPTER 10

BACK TO THE STATES

After V.E. Day, there was a mass movement of men and materials out of the European Theater and back to the U.S. On May 11, 1945, an order from Major General E.E. Partridge, Commanding Officer for the 3rd Air Division, directed the discontinuance of the 862nd Squadron at Debach, England, so the wheels were set in motion. By May 24, 1945, special orders assigned Hann, McEwen, Johnson, and Dersham to a port of debarkation for Trans-Atlantic flight back across the North Atlantic Ocean for an ultimate destination at Boston, MA. With the above crewmembers, the others having been assigned to passage on ships, we also picked up about six pilots from another group who had been flying smaller bombers out of airfields in France, and were anxious to get home.

It was an interesting trip, and as Navigator, the small desk in the nose of our B-17 which served as my workspace became a popular spot. Since the return trip had the same perils involved in earlier Trans-Atlantic crossing, it was quite obvious that some of the passengers, who had never seen me and were concerned about having a safe arrival, were keeping a close watch on my calculations, for whatever purpose that may have served. They all wanted to know where we were, when would we reach Goose Bay, etc. As is usual in that area, the weather was terrible, but we did get across the Atlantic without incident and everyone was happy.

From there we flew to Boston. In early June, the full force of summer hit us like a ton of bricks when we stepped out of that plane. Having been in England for about a year and getting acclimated to those 60 degree below zero temperatures at flight altitude, our blood had thickened to accommodate the change, and Boston seemed like the hottest place on earth – but we were delighted to be there!

After being processed at Boston, we were transferred to Bradley Field in Connecticut, where everyone was split up and shifted to military facilities in their respective sections of the country. McEwen and I went to Fort McPherson, GA, for further processing before being released for 30 days of "rehabilitation, recuperation, and recovery" at home. We all agreed that the Air Force terminology was very appropriate, and everyone needed this time to somewhat unwind. Our departure from McPherson was June 18, 1945.

The old saying "there's no place like home" is certainly true. No pressures, freedom to go where you wanted, when it was convenient, nobody shooting at you, and old friends and acquaintances treating you almost as a hero, all of which helped to loosen up a lot of stress and strain.

At the end of 30 days, I reported to Ellington Field, at Houston, TX. Here I was to be indoctrinated to larger bombers being used in the Pacific Theater of operations, and assigned to further combat duty. It was not a pleasant thought, since military projections for an invasion of Japan anticipated the loss of hundreds of thousands of men in the first assault, and a long drawn out warfare. Fortunately, the atomic bomb solved the problem with the Japanese surrendered. "V.J. Day" (Victory in Japan) celebrated the occasion, and the world thought the problems of future wars had been resolved. How wrong we were!!

After the war I returned to Fernandina. Not many jobs were available, so I started a small hardware store. In 1950, I married a "Georgia Gal," Frances Hollinshead, from Milledgeville. Two years later we had a lovely little girl, Sally, and in 1954 a son, E.J. III, Jim.

During the 1950's, I took a job with Container Corp of America, one of the pulp and paper mills built during the late 1930's. My position was Purchasing agent, with responsibility for buying fuel oil, chemicals, maintenance equipment, and all other materials as required to keep the plant running.

I was elected as a member of the City Commission in 1960 and served for nine years. Five of those years I served as Mayor. Two jobs running concurrently was a lot to handle, and I was glad to become the ex-Mayor in 1969.

In 1981, I took early retirement from Container after 27 years. Since I had my brokers license in real estate, I opened an office and enjoyed that for 14 years.

Many changes have occurred on Amelia Island, with tremendous increase of the population. In the mid 1970's, part of the south end of the island was purchased by the Sea Pines Company, of Hilton Head, South Carolina. It became known as "The Amelia Island Plantation". Later "Summer Beach" was developed in the central part of the island, with both places overlooking the Atlantic Ocean. Later, a beautiful Ritz-Carlton hotel became a part of Summer Beach.

It has been an interesting life, and I have been blessed to have a wonderful family and many great friends. In spite of all previous experiences through life, my worst blow was the death of our son in 1992. "E.J." died from Marfan's syndrome, a birth defect which destroys the cardiovascular system. He was 37 at that time. Looking back, I regret that the topic of my wartime experiences was never discussed with him. He wanted to know everything about his family, and would have dearly loved knowing of his father's 8th Air Force activities as outlined in this book.

As for the crew, we became scattered in 1945. Practically all of the individuals lost contact with each other. In the early part of 1987, the phone rang at our house, and the voice on line inquired "Is this E.J. Johnson, Jr., who flew as Navigator on Hann's crew, 8th Air Force, 1944 & 1945?" I was astounded to be having a conversation with Francis Christmas, our crew chief and top turret gunner. We had not been in contact with each other since 1945! After 42 years, it was startling to be talking to Chris on the phone. We enjoyed a long discussion telling each other what had occurred in our lives during that period. Part of his objective in calling was to suggest that I bring my wife, Frances, to a 490th reunion at Nashville, Tennessee. I agreed to consider, and after telling him how much his call was appreciated, we concluded our discussion.

As time grew closer to the date, Mike Quagliano, our radio operator called, also urging attendance at the Nashville reunion. He had been in contact with some of the others, and knew that Christmas, Cooper, and Dersham would meet him there. They had hoped to have me join them as the 5th member. After some consideration, Fran and I decided to join them, and drove up to Nashville to the hotel where the gathering was located. I went to the check-in counter and was standing beside this fellow who was speaking to the clerk. I immediately recognized his voice and said, "You must be Quagliano!" Somewhat dumbfounded, he looked at me and said, "You must be Johnson!" Neither of us had recognized the other, in spite of several recent phone calls, but bear hugs were in order for this meeting after 42 years.

Our wives were introduced to each other, and we were directed to a huge ball room where the 490th group was gathered. We sat at a vacant table, looking around for any familiar face when, lo and behold, we spotted Cooper and his wife, who joined us. Doug excused himself to get some information at the 490th counter, and didn't come back for a while. Mike and I spotted him across the room talking to two guys, couldn't recognize them, and wondered who they were, but they soon came to our table with their wives. Cooper

Five crew members and wives at 490th Bomb Group Reunion, Nashville, Tenn., May, 1987. (First row-left to right) Dersham, Cooper, Marilyn Quagliano, Beverly Cooper, Francis Christmas and wife, Alberta peeking over shoulder, and Shirley Dersham. (Back row) Mike Quagliano, Fran Johnson and Jim Johnson.

had found Christmas and Dersham. obviously, over that 42 year gap, all of us had changed with the aging process... gray hair, no hair, added weight had really confused our group. All of the wives bonded together like sisters, the guys had a lot to talk about, and it was a wonderful occasion. We had seen many things, had a beautiful private dining room at the Opryland Hotel, toured the sights and thoroughly enjoyed our time there.

In 1989, the 490th reunion was held at Reno, Nevada. All five of the crew, and our wives, checked in at the Peppermill Hotel, which included a large casino. it was a beautiful place, in a very interesting locale. Tour sites such as the Virginia City gold and silver mining town, a fantastic museum of old automobiles, race cars of every type and description, and, of course, beautiful Lake Tahoe provided a wonderful background of history. When we were there, it is my recollection that it was rather cold, and snow caps could be observed on the surrounding mountains.

The Casino was a very popular place when not otherwise involved, and my wife found her favorite spot. The area came to be known as her "station" where the other wives knew how to find her when they too wished to play the "slots". The guys began discussing ways and means to locate other crew members who might still be living, but their whereabouts were unknown. Prior to leaving, we all agreed to locate whoever we could to urge them to join us at future reunions. As all good things come to an end, we said goodbyes and headed back to our homes. It was a great experience.

Plans for the 1990 gathering were set for Myrtle Beach, South Carolina. In the meantime, we had learned that Pat McEwen, our co-pilot, and Jim Morrison, Waist Gunner, had died sometime after returning to the states. Milo Simecek, tail gunner was located, and Ray Hann had finally been found. This meant that 7 of us were still kicking!! Since these survivors were scattered from California to Florida, and our location was just a couple of hundred miles from Myrtle Beach, Fran and I invited all of them to visit Fernandina prior to the scheduled time in South Carolina. Everyone arrived here, except Simecek, who was to meet us there. We arranged for them to stay in condos overlooking the Atlantic, and our beautiful beach. We had a fairly large party one evening to introduce them to many friends, which was very enjoyable to everyone. We have a very outstanding museum covering the history of Amelia Island, which has been occupied by 8 different flags during several hundred years. The museum had a private program for all of us, covering every aspect of things our guests were never aware of, followed by picture taking, etc. Following that, the local newspaper, Fernandina News Leader, considered to be the first in Florida, graciously arranged an audience with the group, followed by a story of all crew members being reunited for the first time in

It was great having Hann join us in Fernandina and Myrtle Beach. Here, he seems pleased to have seven queens surrounding him.

45 years. Everyone had a lot of fun, an experience we all remember.

When we got to Myrtle Beach for the 490th gathering, the necessary check in activities, room assignments at the Sea Mist Resort overlooking the ocean, and other minor details were concluded. Sometime later in the first day, Simecek and his wife arrived, so we had all of our survivors. This area is a very historic section, so there were many tours available to see these interesting spots. Everything was delightful, but our group was particularly interested in the Saturday night banquet. It was there that honors were extended to the individual bomber crews who had the highest number of members in attendance. Our seven survivors were the winners and we were delighted. The next morning, everyone packed bags, said "good-byes", and headed back to their respective homes. It had been another delightful gathering.

In 1994, another 490th B.G. reunion was scheduled at Tampa, Florida. Being relatively close, my wife and I decided to drive the approximately 200 miles, stopping along the way for a mid-day lunch and exploring sections of the Gulf Coast areas we had never before seen. As we neared Tampa, there was a shift in the direction, putting us on a dual lane highway heading west into Tampa. We came up behind a car bearing an Illinois license tag and I looked at Fran "Wouldn't it be something if that happened to be Quagliano?". With our curiosity increasing, I pulled around to the left lane and gradually eased up abreast of the other car. Unbelievable as it sounds, there was Quagliano and his wife Marilyn heading for the 490th group destination. When he looked our way and saw who we were, he had a good laugh over such a coincidence. The other members of our crew came in during that afternoon, and we were pleased to see Hann show up, since he had recently had some health problems. In October 1998, Ray Hann turned 80 – a life span I doubt he ever expected to achieve! Our activities were much the same as prior gatherings, so everyone had a great time. After the Saturday night banquet, everyone departed for home.

There were several other reunions after that date, but unexpected circumstances prevented some of us from attending. Christmas

Six crew members, their wives, and members of Historic Museum of Nassau County, Fernandina Beach, Florida after wonderful program on area. 1990.

died a couple of years thereafter, which was a great loss to each of us. However, we hope that three or four of us may be able to gather at future reunions. While the numbers are dropping in attendance, we started our life together as a crew at Ardomore, just nearby, and perhaps we can go back to see the place.

This picture was taken in May 1990 at a reunion of the 490th Bomb Group, which was held at Myrtle Beach, South Carolina. This was the first time all seven living members had been together since V.E. Day in 1945. Front Row, l. to r.: E.J. Johnson Jr., Ray E. Hann, and Douglas M. Cooper. Back Row, l. to r.: Michael C. Quagliano, Milas Simecek, Francis Christmas, and Arthur Dersham. Deceased: Jim Morrison suffered major problems from combat, was returned to the United States, and died a few years later. Pat McEwen completed combat tours and flew back to the States with other crewmembers after the war ended in 1945, but died some years later.

EPILOGUE

Looking back, hindsight has a degree of clarity about events taking place at specific points in history, as well as seeing very clearly the results of bad decisions previously made.

A primary case in point involves President Franklin D. Roosevelt, who met with Winston Churchill and Stalin, the Russian leader, at a place called "Yalta" sometime before his death on April 12, 1945. The purpose of this gathering was to discuss the division of German territories when the war ended, and how to administer help in rebuilding that nation. Stalin had his agenda, which was to divide Germany into three sections, with each to be controlled by the parties involved, the United States, England, and Russia. Stalin wanted a large part of Berlin and all German territories east of that dividing line extending to Poland, which Russia already controlled. Churchill objected very strenuously, but Roosevelt capitulated to Stalin, so Churchill got voted out. The result of this unfortunate decision became known as the "Cold War", which led to the infamous "Berlin Wall", a strangulation of the German people which triggered the "Berlin Airlift" for supplies of food, coal, and other necessities for survival. The United States and England were again forced into very devastating circumstances, which continued in one form or another for about 40 years. Billions and billions of dollars were needlessly spent, a great loss of lives occurred in the final days before V.E. Day, when General Patton and his forces were ordered to stop and wait at the River Elbe, rather than pushing to meet the Russians, and the whole situation was one of the greatest disasters in history.

Unfortunately, none of these efforts helped to protect the world from future disasters. We have had the Korean War, the Vietnam War, the Persian Gulf War, many conflicts in the European area where countries were overtaken by Hitler and endeavored to resolve local issues, only to become mired in factions murdering other factions because of ideological differences, a complete breakdown of the Russian government, no leadership in the arena of World Foreign Policies, and it just goes on and on. The United States, through the U.N., NATO and other world wide contacts, appears to be the primary police force in almost any world wide outbreaks of conflict. This seems to open the door for continuing military buildup, or letting other nations deal with their own problems. The future depends on leadership and integrity. The veterans of World War II fought that war to preserve those freedoms which had been established over years... to be a guiding light for other nations who yearn for an opportunity to grow and prosper in peace.

Former Senator Bob Dole commented recently that World War II veterans are dying out at a rate of 30,000 per month. Obviously, these role models will not be on hand for indefinite periods in the uncertain future. Hopefully, the generations that follow can meet whatever challanges lie ahead, by achieving a greater understanding of the courage, sacfrice and service exemplified by veterans of World War II.